FROM FIRED ....

.... TO HIRED

The Middle Manager's No Nonsense Guide....

TO JOB SEARCHING IN THE 90's

by Reg Pirie

Ink Ink Publishing

FROM FIRED .... TO HIRED

Published in 1994 by:
Ink Ink Publishing
120 Promenade Circle - Suite 1107
Thornhill, Ontario
Canada L4J 7W9

The author has made every effort to make this book as complete and accurate as possible. It is intended purely as a reference and educational guide for those who are or may be involved in a personal career transition. All names used are purely fictional. Neither the publisher nor the author is expressing legal, financial or other professional opinions and readers should seek expert assistance as dictated by their personal circumstances.

Canadian Cataloguing in Publication Data

Pirie, Reg, 1945 -
       From fired -- -- to hired : the middle manager's nononsense guide to - job searching the 90's

ISBN 0-9698196-0-9

1. Middle managers - Employment. 2. Job Hunting.
3. Career development.   I. Title.
HF5382.7.P57 1994   650.14   C94-930896-X

DEDICATION

To my parents who taught me the value of hard work.

To my wife who has supported me in all my ventures.

To two children who constantly motivate me to impart and share what I have learned.

To an old classmate and life-long friend who unwittingly pushed me into action.

To all of you who, like myself, have had to chart a new direction to find a meaningful and rewarding career.

FOCUS

The adjustment necessary to produce a clear and sharply defined image or area of concentration.

ORGANIZATION

To put in a state of mental competence to perform a task in a well coordinated, consistent, harmonious and systematized fashion.

RESEARCH

To diligently, systematically and carefully inquire or investigate a subject in order to discover or revise facts, theories and applications.

ACTIVITY

The quality of acting promptly, with energy, liveliness, alertness and vigorous action.

TABLE OF CONTENTS

TABLE OF CONTENTS - CONTINUED

PREFACE

So, you have officially joined the alumni of the unemployed middle manager. Not that you actively sought out membership in this club - one with the fastest growing roster of new nominees. By the time you have reached the decision to purchase this book, you have likely come to the conclusion that the job search game has changed dramatically since you first entered the work force.

Some of you will have graduated from high school in the 50's and 60's and after landing your first full-time job, you started to climb the proverbial ladder of success. Lots of hard work, the occasional bit of good luck and a great deal of stick-to-itiveness allowed you to progress into the ranks of middle management or beyond.

Others of you will have slightly different backgrounds. As accessibility to higher education improved in the 60's and 70's, more and more people were entering the work force, tightly clutching an almost magical piece of parchment proclaiming academic excellence, or at the very least academic persistence.

No, the diploma did not come with a guarantee for success, but for many it opened doors of opportunity allowing almost immediate entrance into the ranks of management. For other college and university graduates, their education helped to position them on accelerated corporate training programs which again allowed rapid access to good career options within middle and upper management.

And what of the latest new breed to join the management team? Emerging throughout the 80's, graduate students rapidly moved into the already swollen ranks of management, armed with superior educations. The MBAs not only brought with them higher educational credentials, but they also represented a wave of exciting new business concepts. Corporations were thirsting for anything and anyone to help capitalize on the opportunities presented by the boom times of the 80's. Expansion, globalization, acquisitions, mergers and a host of other trendy terminology all boiled down to the simple reality of business life - maximizing bottom line profits.

For a period of time, all three categories worked in relative harmony. While ideas and concepts sometimes clashed, there appeared to be room for everyone in this large cadre of management personnel. And why not? Career progression was reasonably assured regardless of whether you had started in the "mail room", the lowest level on the management ladder or if you had been catapulted into more senior echelons by virtue of your graduate degree.

That is not to say there were not minor pitfalls along the way. Cyclic economic vagaries periodically stalled upward movement, personal setbacks might have delayed advancement and on occasion, other outside factors like mergers and acquisitions temporarily impeded career progression.

But by the end of the 80's a sense of foreboding began to filter into the business world. The earlier buoyant years had heightened profit expectations and in a mad scramble, corporations started to do everything and anything to maintain profits. As the recession deepened, thoughts of maintaining revenues were quickly replaced with the damage control mentality of curtailing costs. As we all know the biggest cost factor in any business is people!

Reorganization, downsizing, rightsizing, divestitures, reengineering and any number of other newly coined phrases were rapidly being added to the lexicon of each and every corporation. Many survived wave after wave of staff reductions and reorganizations.

Eventually, change caught up with you and through no particular fault of your own, you are now faced with a harsh reality - the difficult task of seeking out new employment. Others of you are waiting and teetering on the brink, but you are no longer satisfied with your own inaction and you want to take back some control and prepare for your next career move.

And what is the purpose of all this negative rhetoric at the beginning of a book which is intended to aid you in landing a new job? Well, there are three primary reasons. First, it is important to recognize and fully appreciate that the world has not singled you out as the only person who is without a job. Second, there is a need to face the reality that you are up against a great deal of competition. Finally, there is only one person who can land a job for you - **and that person is you!**

Everyone else can only hinder you or help you. And that is where this no-nonsense book comes into play. This publication does not come with a guarantee. What it does offer is some pragmatic and practical insight about the job search process which will allow you to edge out many who are competing for a diminishing number of employment opportunities.

The rest is up to you and you alone.

"Get your happiness out of your work,

or you will never know what happiness is."

- Elbert Hubbard

Chapter 1

INTRODUCTION

As you leafed through the first few pages of this book, you encountered four words and four definitions.

- Focus
- Organization
- Research
- Activity

If you want to succeed in your job search you will need to constantly reflect on those words. You must turn those words into actions. Before taking a look at the job search process, it is important to understand and appreciate why Focus, Organization, Research and Activity are so important.

Focus

For the most part, our lives are filled with minor ups and downs but generally speaking we feel in control under normal circumstances. Job loss can take away that sense of control and most people do not realize how many factors come into play. It is not just the loss of a job that you have to contend with but there are a host of other issues which need to be faced before you can even begin to effectively seek out new opportunities.

Unless you come to grips with all of these matters in an orderly fashion, you are not going to be in a position to run an effective job search campaign. In reality there are two parts to the focusing process. First you need to address personal matters and second you want to reach an informed decision about what you want to do in your next career. Do not kid yourself - these two phases must be handled separately and you will do yourself and your family a disservice if you attempt to reverse the order.

Organization

Organization is a simple word but one that every business person has heard, seen and used since first stepping over the corporate threshold. If you reflect upon each and every performance review you have completed for your subordinates and indeed for every evaluation done on your own performance, chances are the expression "organizational skills / abilities" will have surfaced.

There are many definitions which can be applied but by virtue of its frequent inclusion in the business vocabulary, you can be assured of the ongoing importance of this seemingly over used word.

If you attached significance to the word in your previous life, it will soon take on even a more profound emphasis as you begin your job search. You will discover, there are several phases to the job search process but threaded throughout the entire procedure is an inherent need to be organized and to keep organized.

When it comes to the ability to be organized, people generally fall in three categories. Those who seem to have a natural inclination, those who have learned through the rigors of business life and those who can not or will not place an importance on this concept. If you fall into the latter grouping, take a word of advice - be prepared to get organized!

In fact, this book will help you see the criticality of being well organized and it will offer you some simplistic suggestions. These observations will not only assist you in your job search but they can easily be carried over into your next career.

Research

For the vast majority of people, this word provokes little reaction unless you come from a business background requiring intensive checking of facts, figures and historical data. Generally speaking, most of us do not have a natural or acquired tendency to accumulate information, other than that which may be directly linked to a job or project.

When you are in the job search mode, you are constantly faced with situations where you must be knowledgeable about facts and different scenarios. You will want to know about people, companies, projects, new initiatives, changes, future directions and other wide ranging bits of data which will facilitate effective networking.

A large number of people discount the importance of research, perhaps because it is foreign or likely because it conjures up images associated with mundane work which can be glossed over to quickly move forward to more meaningful endeavours. Not so!

Research is really as easy as reading a newspaper or dusting off your library card. The tricky part about research is being sufficiently focused and organized to know what is valuable and essential to your job search. In the most basic terms, you have to re-learn how to read, listen and watch.

The greatest plus about research is that most of it is either free or cheap. Flipping on the daily business report on television costs you virtually nothing. Strolling into your local library will cost you next to nothing and purchasing any of the business newspapers will cost the staggering sum of something less than a dollar. Sound too pricey? Give up seven cigarettes a day, your cup of coffee at the neighborhood deli or a can of your favorite soft drink.

We will get into newspaper reading in more depth but for now, make a couple of personal commitments. First, you are going to purchase a paper every day and second, you are going to learn how to read it from start to finish - with a view to researching.

Like organization, research should be and must be intertwined throughout your entire job search process.

Activity

Of the four major elements in an effective job search, activity perhaps edges out the others by a few percentage points. Maybe purposeful activity might be a better expression but in any event, you can be focused, superbly organized and well researched but you are not apt to find a job if you do not get it in gear!

Take a moment to reflect back on your last position. What were your posted hours? What were your average real hours? How much time did you spend commuting to and from the work place? Stop right now, grab a pencil and paper and truthfully calculate the amount of time you previously spent working or in work related situations, including the commute and business trips.

Got the figure? Now discount the number by 15%, purely because everyone exaggerates the number of hours they truly work. Whether the weekly total is sixty hours or thirty hours, you have just established a benchmark for the amount of time you should be expending as a self-employed job seeker.

Face it, for the next few months you are a true entrepreneur and your product or service is you. You are the boss and you set the guidelines and time frames for this all important project.

The balance of this book is dedicated to helping you, help yourself. It will get you focused, keep you organized, direct you in your research and cause you to remain purposefully active until you land your desired job.

Before you do anything else, read this book from cover to cover and then read it again.

"Initiative is doing the right thing...

without being told."

                                        - Elbert Hubbard

Chapter 2

FOCUS & FEELINGS

The next four chapters are devoted to the issue of focusing. Achieving a focus may in the first instance sound like a process to bring you to a singular, high resolution conclusion. Indeed, that is not entirely true as most of us have several factors at work in our lives at any one moment and by extension, we have many issues to focus upon. The best possible scenario occurs when all these elements have clarity and purpose.

The entire focusing process is much more involved than people generally anticipate and the reason is apt to stem from the fact that many equate focusing solely with decisions surrounding a job objective. Unfortunately, life does not come equipped with a built-in auto focus feature like the newest high-tech camcorder. As such, we all must be prepared to make some manual adjustments, both from a personal and work perspective.

Before dealing with the various major segments in arriving at focused decisions, let me introduce a graphic entitled the "Future Focus" which will better illustrate not only the subject of this chapter but also the whole job search concept.

FUTURE FOCUS

START

FOCUS

DEALING WITH DEPARTURE, FAMILY ISSUES
FINANCIAL, LEGAL, SETTLEMENTS
ASSESSMENT, SELF ASSESSMENT
ABILITIES / SKILLS REVIEW
ACCOMPLISHMENTS
STRENGTHS

ORGANIZATION   CAREER OBJECTIVE (S)

RESEARCH   RESUME (S)
                         BUSINESS PLAN

ACTIVITY

SEARCH STRATEGY, CAMPAIGN PLAN
VERIFICATION, FOCUS ADJUSTMENT
INTERVIEWING TECHNIQUES
NEGOTIATING, INTERVIEWS
RESEARCH, NETWORKING
INFORMATION MEETINGS
LETTER WRITING
CAREER ADS

LANDING

ON GOING CAREER MANAGEMENT

In the most straight forward situations, there is a start and a finish to any procedure. From your vantage point, the start is the beginning of your job search (where you are today) and the finish is new employment (where you want to be as soon as possible). Between those two points you must deal with a multitude of issues and you must undertake several initiatives to arrive at the desired end result.

One approach is to throw everything into a hopper and wait for a job to emerge at the bottom. That might be workable in the most simplistic of cases but you are involved in a traumatic upheaval in your life which calls for a mechanism to bring some semblance of order to a potentially chaotic situation. The "Future Focus" illustration is intended to offer a visual depiction of how this process works and why it is necessary to involve a more step by step methodology.

In essence, the "Future Focus" graphic allows you to manage your job search by segregating the process into three major events. The upper portion is primarily dedicated to focusing, allowing you to systematically deal with:

-        Your history and your previous employer
-        Immediate complications of job loss
-        Family and personal issues
-        Future career directions
-        Arriving at a career objective

A clear focus on a career objective actually becomes a distillation of all the items you have dealt with in the focusing stage of your job search. Once you have reached this point, you can effectively develop a resume stating:

-        Who you are
-        What you want to do
-        What you have accomplished

-        What quantifies your accomplishments

Armed with your well-informed decisions, generated by taking the time to get focused and supported by a professionally crafted resume, you are then ready to tackle the actual campaign which needs to be mounted to find a job.

The lower segment denotes the wide variety of tasks which must be undertaken to exploit the job market. It is this final phase which people generally equate to the job search but as can be seen by the illustration, it is only one piece of the entire puzzle.

Let me repeat an earlier comment. It is extremely doubtful that you will run an effective job search campaign if you insist on leaping forward to the latter phases, without taking the time to get focused.

If you insist on making this error, you run the risk of not finding a job and at best, you will land a position which you will ultimately end up disliking. Like most things in life, do it properly the first time. Invest some energy and thought in focusing.

Feelings and Emotions

The most immediate sensation after losing a job is a wide range of emotions and feelings. Volumes have been written on the subject of how to deal with the initial emotions and realities of a job loss. And the one truism which is consistent throughout every article, book or reassuring word is the fact that you must eventually put these issues behind you if you are ever to summon up the energy, drive and tenacity required to mount a proper job search campaign.

Unfortunately, no one has ever developed a step by step procedure which allows you to stroke off each issue to be dealt with, preparatory to moving on to the next agenda item. To be candid, you might just as well accept a few facts. The old expression about experiencing an emotional roller coaster ride is true. Indeed, if you have a significant other or if you have children, regardless of their ages, they too will be joining you on the this ride which has highs and lows.

As suggested earlier, there is no 1-2-3 formula but let's start by looking at the more typical feelings which you are apt to encounter. Just for the record, the intent of this commentary is not to diminish or resolve these feelings but rather, it is to give you some understanding of the major phases which you will experience.

Being able to identify and gauge where you are at on the roller coaster can be a significant asset in helping you maintain control and in moving forward.

Feelings and Emotions - Shock

No matter how well prepared we are for the possibility of severance, the simple fact remains when it is finally communicated, there is a definite sense of shock. All the posturing about being ready for such an event does little to soften the blow when the news is finally delivered and words or thoughts such as "It can't really be happening to me!" just naturally leap to mind.

Bewilderment is perhaps the most descriptive word which can be applied to this feeling and there are varying degrees of a sense of true loss. Not only are you dealing with your own situation but in many instances you are also confronted by the fact that several of your co-workers have been impacted as well.

As is the case with the shock associated in medical situations, there are steps which can be taken to accelerate your recovery (both in the short term and in the long term) and we will address many of these in the chapter on coping.

The most important thing to remember is that you are very likely to experience this feeling and you are not the only person in the world who is faced with the disorientation brought about by shock.

A word of caution. If you have a history of depression or if you have been treated in the past for stress-related illness, do not delay in communicating with your family physician. This is no time to become a stoic. You want to avoid any complications which could impede your future ability to get on with your job search.

Feelings and Emotions - Anger

Like shock, anger is a natural reaction which is often focused toward your previous employer, a specific boss, uncooperative subordinates, seemingly non supportive family members or more likely yourself, for allowing this event to happen.

Under normal circumstances, we do not associate anger with any positive connotations but in small doses it can be a powerful antibiotic in the healing process. Let me be clear, this is not a reference to destructive rage directed at yourself or others around you. On the other hand, there is a natural surge of energy associated with anger and if you are capable of harnessing that raw power, it can propel your job search activities.

For those who are prone to having a short fuse, the anger stage can pass quickly and they typically progress to the acceptance level in fairly short order. Others, who are not accustomed to dealing with this emotion, can experience difficulty in venting anger. If left unchecked, this pent up fury can have devastating long-term negative implications, resulting in a very exasperating job search.

If you see yourself falling in the latter category, you should pay particular attention to the various ways and means of coping.

Feelings and Emotions - Acceptance

You do not have to like what has happened to you! The reality is you may never fully agree with the so-called fairness and equity of the actions or circumstances surrounding your job loss. What you do need to do is to come to grips with the plain and simple truth that your job is no longer there. Dwelling on what could have been or what might have been or what should have been, will not aid you in moving forward with your job search.

Actually, the latter statements are not entirely true as you will find when we come to the self assessment phase. But at this juncture, it is critical that you move toward accepting the reality, recognizing that looking backward is not going to enhance your chances for landing a job.

Feelings and Emotions - Fear

Under normal circumstances, fear creeps into the equation somewhere between anger and acceptance. Job loss for any reason can have a devastating impact on self-confidence, regardless of why you have been let go. Even if you have been caught up in the ever increasing number of company reorganizations and downsizings, there is always a degree of self-doubt that manifests itself when you lose your job.

Fear can take on many forms. Primarily you can fear the prospects of finding alternate employment - more simply put, "What happens if I can't find a job!" But we all have other personal concerns that become magnified when we are forced into dealing with new situations. To better understand why fear is such a factor and one which has to be dealt with, take a moment to reflect on some of the job search related activities which cause many of us a great deal of anxiety. How often have you fretted as the following statements have raced through your mind at three in the morning:

"I have never been any good at job interviews."

"I hate writing letters. How am I going to reply to career ads and compete with all the hot shots."

"I know that I have to get out and meet people but I have never been outgoing."

"My educational qualifications are not great. What if they are not good enough?"

"I have friends who are better qualified than I am and they have been out of work for a year or more."

"Everyone says you have to sell yourself and I despise selling at the best of times."

"How will this impact on the family and are we going to have to significantly alter our life style?"

In times of job loss, you often hear people talking about shock, anger or acceptance. Fear is not a word that frequently slides into these conversations and that is a shame. The fact that others avoid mentioning this little four letter word can cause you to assume you are the only person who is truly apprehensive or downright scared about the prospects of being unemployed and tackling the job market.

So prepare yourself and your family to deal with the emotional roller coaster. Some or all of the above feelings may apply to you and the important thing to remember is most people harbour these feelings. And even of greater importance is the fact these concerns can be overcome if you have some help, support and a personal plan of attack.

Chapter 3

FOCUS & DECISIONS

Having tentatively acknowledged the fact you may be experiencing some of the feelings noted in Chapter Two, you will
soon be exposed to the next reality. You will be thrust into many
situations which require almost immediate decisions on your part.
In the vast majority of cases you are going to be faced with choices
which you have previously not encountered and you will be
inundated with well meaning advice from family and friends.

The choices revolve around the more pragmatic issues such as
possible legal actions and dealing with short or long-term financial
decisions. You will be confronted by mountains of paper
concerning pensions, stock option plans, releases and settlement
payments.

Financial

Financial decisions appear to be pushed upon you within the first
ten minutes during the notification of your severance. While we
might all prefer to have a little time to absorb the reality of the job

loss, the fact remains we would all be crying foul if an employer did not include settlement details and options with a termination letter.

Those daunting letters deserve at least one or two paragraphs, given they are the first item which can cause you to lose control over your own destiny. Who writes these rambling pieces of prose? The answer to that question might provide you with some insight about why they take so long to digest.

Rest assured, your ex-employer's lawyers had a hand in preparing the covering letter, as well as many of the attachments. This is not intended to be a slight against the legal profession but when have you ever absorbed the essence of any of their documents at first glance?

Next, you will find that the personnel or human resource department has added a few editorial comments to include a degree of sensitivity in an otherwise dehumanizing process. In all likelihood, they have also been charged with the responsibility of capturing and articulating the implications associated with all the compensation and benefit issues.

Finally, and the most mystifying of all, is the page or two inserted about pensions, stock options and RSP's. If the other correspondence has not confused you, the latter will defy comprehension, at least until the fifth reading and even then, you will have more questions than answers. My apologies to most of the pension departments but the KISS philosophy (Keep It Simple Stupid) is obviously not a concept ascribed to in the rarefied air of pension administration.

To add further insult to injury, the last page of these typical packages of overwhelming information is likely a release form which categorically states in bold print that you are to sign and return the form within ten days or two weeks, or even sooner.

If the foregoing comments seem uncomplimentary and flip, they are! Human nature being what it is, you will undoubtedly attempt to hastily read the severance letter as your boss is informing you about your departure. You will make another valiant effort in the car or on the bus and perhaps by the third reading at home, you may be grasping some of the rules and regulations which are being imposed upon you.

If one paragraph in this book should be underlined because it pertains to the first day or two of your new found status as an unemployed person, the following would receive such treatment:

<u>The best advice is to set the letter aside until the next morning. Failing that, at least start to jot down what you do not understand and above all, sign nothing until those questions have all been resolved and you have sought out professional help.</u>

Several factors influence the amount of a settlement and legislative requirements are first and foremost. Many employers go beyond the legal requirements and make a genuine effort to compensate for other factors like tenure, age and potential difficulty in securing new employment. Legal concerns will be dealt with in the next section but for now, let's deal with financial matters.

Whether your employer is offering a bare bones minimum settlement or a more generous arrangement, you are faced with numerous decisions and options. Making a quick and uninformed choice can lead to negative implications which could significantly influence your future financial stability.

Most people react to job loss by immediately enacting sweeping cost cutting measures, insuring that each penny is doled out with miserly care. It is tough to argue against such prudence but spending a little time and money in seeking out and securing the advice of a good financial planner will be one of your better investments.

Before you run out and see a lawyer or before you start editing your dusty resume, stop and consider where you can find a some reputable input about finances. And no, that does not mean a fifteen minute chat with your local bank manager! A few of you might have already engaged a financial planner and your task just became infinitely easier. For those who do not have one, get on the phone and start to make some inquiries through friends, relatives and business associates.

If you are new to the whole world of financial planning, take the time to phone and talk with three or four planners before you decide to see any of them. Here are a few hints in terms of what you should research before you even walk into an office:

1.   Do they have a solid reputation? Clearly the best way to verify this is through someone you trust. The good planners will not try pressure tactics to get you in the door.

2.   Are they knowledgeable when it comes to severance settlements and various related tax implications? Most are but even excellent planners are not always accustomed to dealing with these special issues.

3.   Are they accessible and able to meet with you in a timely fashion, bearing in mind some of the restraints imposed by your former employer? Pose the pointed question.

4.   Does the planner encourage an initial meeting to establish a rapport with you and your spouse? If they do not raise the issue of spousal involvement, further questioning is warranted. In most cases this is a family matter, requiring considerable deliberation by both partners. You may not be handing over your cash to this person but you are going to be acting upon their advice. As such, you should have a genuine comfort level with the planner.

5.   Ask if they are prepared to discuss possible avenues available to replace lost or soon to be lost benefits? A good financial planner does not deal exclusively with cash items but also with those other aspects of your family's financial well being which do not necessarily show up on the balance sheet.

6.   And what about Unemployment Insurance? A sobering thought this early in the game but financial planners who are in tune with people in transition should be able to offer counsel on this subject and respond to questions arising from the implications brought about via various types of severance payments.

7.   How much is all this going to cost? In all fairness, it is difficult for any consultant to answer that question without an exploratory meeting but at least you can determine the cost, if any, for the first one hour of discussions.

There is a limit to what a financial planner can accomplish with the monetary resources you have available. But by seeking out professional advice at the outset, you can start to formulate a plan of attack that may directly influence how you proceed with your job search.

Armed with this information, you begin to regain control and you are positioned to make some informed decisions about accepting your settlement or choosing to begin some form of negotiation, where this latter course is deemed reasonable.

Legal

Over the course of the past ten or fifteen years, we have seen the media coverage about severance settlements blossom into an almost daily occurrence, complete with banner headlines ranging from "Employees Shafted" to "Another Golden Parachute Unfurls!"

In reality, these two extremes do exist but take a moment to reflect on how many people have lost jobs in the 80's and 90's. How often, do you hear or read about the average individual? Everyone would like just a little bit more and it is always easy to self-justify why your case is different.

The previous statement should not be misconstrued. It is not intended to advocate for a minute that you should blithely accept whatever is offered to you. There are a variety of circumstances which warrant questioning and research.

The first thing you must consider is your previous employer. Have they had a long history of being faced with work force reductions? If they have, chances are reasonably good that they have developed a firm set of guidelines, intended to cover almost every eventuality. You can also assume such employers have sought out professional counsel concerning the legalities and perhaps even the moralities of their severance policy.

That said, these are times of significant upheaval in any organization and it is not uncommon to encounter situations where unique circumstances have been overlooked or forgotten, either intentionally or unintentionally. Obviously, if you have an outstanding written contract with a company, it may well supersede the more traditional settlement formulas.

Similarly, if the company recently enticed you away from another employer, that factor may influence settlement calculations. In a third scenario, if you were granted "acknowledged tenure" with another firm which was involved in a merger with or acquisition by your latest employer, that too may require further consideration.

<u>May</u> is a key word in the above two paragraphs anu your worst line of attack is to assume anything. Some of the more pro-active companies delineate just how they have arrived at your overall settlement figure and they have no qualms about spelling it out in your termination letter. Others, although fair or generous, only outline the legal requirements and tend to lump the residual payments under the broad heading such as "without prejudice and in recognition for past contributions."

And finally, you still have some companies which fervently believe in the basic premise of the barter system. That mentality often starts with a low ball offer, followed by a "wait and see" posture. Frankly, the latter situation is the most perplexing and the most time consuming, for both parties.

The following advice is provided for the majority of cases and does not reflect action which should be contemplated in extraordinary situations. The steps are predicated on common sense but face it, common sense does not always prevail in the first few days following a termination.

Step One

You will find in most severance letters that a company suggests a contact person within the organization who you can communicate with relative to technical questions. The truth be known, your previous boss or your boss's boss is not necessarily trying to avoid you. It is more likely than not that they know little about the complexities of the company's severance policies. Does it not make some sense to start by asking someone who understands the stated rules and procedures?

Assuming you are not totally satisfied with your settlement, take the time to reflect on the issues of concern and write out your specific questions. Then call the suggested contact person but do not pick up the phone until you are under control. Remember, the person you are going to speak with is the policy interpreter and they are not likely to have the ultimate authority to change anything. Your mission during this call it to determine the company's stated policy or perhaps their going in position. This is the time for clarification, not confrontation.

Step Two

With the information in hand from step one, you are at your first crossroads. If you are reasonably comfortable with the settlement and the subsequent explanations, you can choose to sign off and get underway with the future.

That is very much a personal decision and may be influenced by the historical fairness and equity attributed to your employer. Simply put, there are some employers in the market place which are known for exceptionally generous settlements and as such, their willingness to negotiate is extremely limited.

Step Three

If you have not been fortunate enough to work for this type of organization, you may have some nagging questions. Stop right there! You need to satisfy yourself about the appropriateness of the settlement and the answers to those questions can not be found by talking to friends, relatives or previous co-workers. You need a professional!

That professional is not simply a lawyer. Like most professions, the legal system has a wide variety of specialists and what you do not need is a generalist. Chances are that your personal lawyer who handled your last mortgage or will, is not fully equipped to address your employment law questions.

Your previous employer has undoubtedly engaged a qualified legal expert - do yourself a favor and do the same thing. A little research and a few phone calls will easily put you in touch with a pro. One other important piece of advice, you do not get professional counsel for nothing. If you are concerned enough to look for help, you should be willing to fork out the $300 or $400 for an hour of consultation. The numerous criteria noted for selecting a good financial planner are basically the same as those you want to utilize in engaging a lawyer.

You are paying for the lawyers advice so prepare yourself by jotting down certain pertinent facts before you even pick up the phone. A sampling of the commonly asked questions is recorded below:

- Ex-employers name:
- Position last held:
- Date you assumed the position:
- Was your last internal move a promotion?
- Base salary upon departure:
- Date of severance notice:
- Were there any incentive bonuses and if so:
    - How much and how often?
    - How were they determined?
- Performance history:
- Stated reason for termination:
- Total tenure and amount of settlement:
- Settlement calculation formula:
- Method and timing of payment:
- Caveats on lump sum payments - if any:
- Allowances for lost benefits - if any:
- Benefit continuation stipulations:
- Arrangements for retirement options:
- Arrangements regarding fringe benefits:
    - Leased vehicles, memberships etc.

This is not the time to be cheap! If you are not fully satisfied about the equity of your settlement, you are not going to be able to concentrate on the future. Take the time and spend the money for qualified advice.

Step Four

Accept the direction of the professional after carefully weighing the potential value of the possible gain, against the distraction of not being able to move forward with total concentration and commitment to your job search.

Both financial and legal decisions rest with you and you alone. Whichever direction you choose, you are again taking back control of your own situation.

Chapter 4

FOCUS & COPING

Recognizing this situation could well be foreign to you and your family, just how do you cope on a daily basis? If you felt you had a modicum of control over your life in the past, how do you go about regaining some of that control to maintain your own sanity and also to help yourself prepare for one of the most important jobs in your life - the challenge of finding a job?

Chapter Two touched on some of the feelings which often manifest themselves immediately following the loss of a job. And in those first few hours or even days, many people simply "make it through" with little or no regard for how they are going to cope with the day-to-day rigors of temporarily being without work.

For some, this is an unpleasant repeat of a past experience and for countless others, it is a first time confrontation with an unwanted vacation which has no date of return. While it is never wise to generalize, people do tend to fit into certain stereotypical pigeon holes during the first week of unemployment. There is not a "right or wrong" or "better or worse" pigeon hole but most people will resemble one of the following:

LEAVE ME ALONE....

Either by word or gesture, this person just wants to think and re-think. In fact, there is a desire to replay their own work history in an effort to identify some historic event or personal decision which may have ultimately caused the job loss.

Sometimes the "Leave me alone...." type will come up with a legitimate reason and more often than not, they reach an equally true conclusion that they made no glaring career errors and their job loss was beyond their own control. Generally, these are the same people who will want to formulate a skeleton plan of attack for the future before returning to normal.

I JUST WANT TO RELAX AND DO NOTHING....

This is another common response and should not be confused with the "Leave me alone...." reaction. In this era of the high pressure business environment, several people have been working in overdrive for extended periods of time. To them, job loss offers a temporary haven, an opportunity to let the body and the mind recharge.

Immediately taking a three week vacation when you lose your job is not generally seen as a wise move, simply because it is far too easy to slip into the avoidance mode. Once that happens, it is extremely difficult to become motivated to start an all out job search campaign. Similarly, without reaching some decisions about career objectives before you start a real vacation, you run the risk of having an ineffective holiday because you are still worried about not being in control of your own situation - or at least what direction you are headed in.

In short, there is nothing wrong with "I just want to relax and do nothing...." types but this approach should not last beyond a week and then languish into an undefined, over extended vacation period.

STAND BACK,
I'VE GOT A MILLION THINGS TO DO....

We all know people who at the best of times can be described as perpetual motion machines. In fact, people with longer lasting degrees of anger quite often fit in this category.

Without exaggeration, this is the type of person who is up at dawn the day following their severance and by 8:00 A.M. he or she has a new resume drafted. By 9:30 a call has been made to a lawyer and the financial planner. And by 10:00 they have rushed out to buy this book!

Literally, during the first week they have cleaned the garage, painted the spare room, detailed both cars and reorganized the basement. All kidding aside, this person thrives on activity and they simply have to maintain this momentum because by slowing down or stopping, they know they are going to feel defeated and perhaps lost.

Again, there is no right or wrong and as soon as this type of person can focus these high energy levels toward the job search, they will truly begin to feel as though they are back in control.

I AM READY TO START,
BUT WHERE DO I BEGIN....

Not everyone is the deep thinker, the relaxer or the whirlwind. Some people move very quickly toward the acceptance level and simply want to get on with their lives and the process of finding a new job. And that willingness or readiness can be a big plus, if you know where to begin and what to do. In fact, the first three categories eventually reach this state of mind and all four types become ready to tackle the task at hand, the job of finding a job!

What has been described in the above few paragraphs are not coping mechanisms but rather, they are the outward reactions of how a large number of people may respond immediately following a severance.

The following section is intended to give you greater insight about things you can do to better cope with stresses and changes brought about by a job loss. These are suggestions only and this is not a tick-list of activities which you run through once and then proclaim "There, I am finished, I've done everything required to cope with my situation until I land a new job!"

These are just a few ideas which may be of assistance and you will find that as is the case with most good ideas, they need constant cultivation and care.

Family Support

It is impossible to speak to each and every family scenario. Statistically, readers of this book are likely to be married, with a couple of children and perhaps the family pet. For those of you who do not fall in this neatly prepackaged example, the following common sense observations may also have applicability to you.

If there is an advantage derived from the ballooning number of management severances during the past ten years, it is the fact that the negative stigma attached to job loss has diminished or almost disappeared. Gone are the days when someone faked the daily trudge to the office while trying to summon up the courage to tell a spouse.

Likewise, spouses have had media information heaped upon them about the changes within the job market and potential consequences. Even in uncommunicative families, it is quite likely there has been a discussion surrounding the topic of "What would we do if this happened to us?"

All this to say the degree of spousal support has not really changed over the years but the amount of pre-conditioned understanding has. And how does all of this fit into coping? When it comes to coping, you will soon find the most crucial and most effective aid to you, your spouse and your family is through communication. That's right, plain old fashioned talking!

Oddly enough, the high pressure jobs of the 80's and 90's can be blamed in part for poor family communications. How often have you heard phrases like:

>"Don't bring your work home with you!"

>"I don't want to talk about the office, I just want to relax tonight!"

>"I don't have time to talk tonight, I have to get this report done by tomorrow morning!"

We have been conditioned to avoid talking about work-related issues and since there is a natural correlation between job loss and work, we can easily fall into the trap of not communicating with a spouse or family about anything which even hints of being job search related.

Communication requires a massive effort on your part. You need to take the first step and this needs to go well beyond blurting out "I got sacked today!" Every relationship is different but if there is ever a time when you need to force yourself to express your feelings, thoughts and concerns, it is when you are in the job search mode.

Do not forget, you have lost not only your job but also a venue to communicate. You will soon discover there is a burning need to simply chat with someone and you no longer have an office surrounding which in the past facilitated the natural inclination to converse with people. In large measure, that void must be initially filled by communicating at home. If you do open the communication doors do not be surprised if you overhear the children commenting on the unexpected and unusual amount of dialogue within the home.

On the other side of the coin, you have a spouse and children who are concerned about you and are eager to know what is going on. Do not be selfish! Job loss does not only affect you. It has a far reaching impact on all those around you.

Remember the earlier remarks about the infamous severance letters? Sharing those convoluted sentences and paragraphs with a spouse can be a great catalyst to re-opening the lines of communication. You need options and thoughts to help you formulate action plans and what better person to ask than someone who knows you better than most?

That reliance on spousal input should not stop after the first few days. Your spouse should be involved in the financial planning process and in any legal discussions. As you move forward in your actual job search, spouses can be a great source of advice and can act as a sounding board for your ideas.

And what about the children? If you have not already come to the realization that kids today are infinitely smarter than we ever were, you will undoubtedly discover this when you are unemployed.

A friend of mine was laid off and sought my advice the next day. During the course of that conversation, I asked if he and his wife had told their two boys, ages 5 and 7. The answer was "Not yet, but we will get around to it when we have come to grips with the situation ourselves." My response was to do it now but my friend chose to delay.

A few days later he confided in me again and said he had been shocked when his eldest son had asked him out of the blue if he had been fired. After stumbling through a less than eloquent or well-rehearsed explanation, my friend inquired as to how the boys had come to this conclusion.

The answer was simple and the oldest son's dialogue went something like this: "Our buddy down the street asked if we were going on vacation because he had seen you at home and when I said no, he suggested that when his Dad was home but not holidaying, he had been fired!"

A true story and all the more reason to sharpen your family communication skills. Children at all ages need honest input and assurances. Those can range from confirming that Fido (the family hound) will still be fed to much more serious questions about the affordability of university.

Do not underestimate the true strength of the family unit and reciprocate by keeping them involved and informed.

Friends

Friendships range from a casual acquaintance to someone who can be described as a true brother or sister. In the case of the latter, these people might be as supportive and as important to you as your family in terms of coping during your job search.

Most of us enjoy a range of friendships but you could well be faced with a strange reaction from some people and this response deserves clarification. At a seminar recently conducted for a group of people who had been laid off, the question was posed about the reactions they had received from friends. In the first 30 seconds we had noted words and phrases like supportive, shocked, dismayed, worried and angry.

After the initial flurry of responses a hush fell on the crowd and finally one brave soul spoke up and used the word "avoidance" to describe what he had felt. Again, another pause and then several chimed in that, they too, had sensed this same uncomfortable vibration from some people who they would normally have seen as being very supportive and caring.

The stark realization is many people do not know how to respond when a friend or acquaintance has lost a job. It is a well-overused analogy but broaching this subject is often akin to offering condolences about a death in the family.

It can be very easy to assume the posture that you are the impacted individual and why should you shoulder the extra burden of helping your friends deal with your loss. One option is to take that stance but you run the real risk of losing or diminishing a sound friendship.

You need the support of all your friends to assist you in coping and if you want to be more pragmatic, these are the people who could well become strong supporters as you begin to network toward a new job. While it may not seem to be fair, right or proper, you have a responsibility and an obligation to yourself to bridge any gap which may become evident.

This is not that difficult - a simple phone call explaining your situation, with no strings attached, is usually all that is needed. "Susan, I suspect you have heard some rumors and I just wanted to let you know that I am no longer with ABC. Right now I am tidying up a few loose ends and I intend to get underway with my job search next week."

You are demonstrating that you value the friendship enough to inform them personally about your situation, you are indicating you have a preliminary plan and you are not making any overtures asking for a job. The most common response is apt to be an offer to help and your best reaction is to thank the individual and suggest you will get back to them when you are in a better position to ask for their specific assistance and input.

Like family, good friends will be supportive and concerned. They will want to help and you should be willing to accept those genuine gestures. Maintaining good friendships also allows you and your family to retain some normalcy in your day-to-day living, whether it be a Saturday barbecue, the mid-week outing to little league or the annual family trek to the zoo.

One last point to ponder when it comes to friendships. You will soon discover or re-discover that many of your associates have experienced what you are going through. They are part of the new alumni and as such, they can offer first-hand advice about what to do and what not to do. In the case of these members of the new order, you will find most of them are the first to come forward with unsolicited words of encouragement.

Hobbies and Volunteer Work

Just what is a hobby and why do we have hobbies? The most straight forward definition is an activity or pursuit designed to provide one with pleasure and relaxation. If there was ever a time when pleasure and relaxation were high on the list of priorities, it would be while you are grappling with the stresses, strains and exasperations associated with a job search.

Hobbies are a diversion and if you are treating your search like work, you are as much in need of a pleasant distraction now, as you ever were while climbing the corporate ladder.

As one job seeking executive mused, "Years ago I did every bit of carpentry work around the house. Then, I didn't have the time to do it but I had the money to get the work done for me. Now I just enjoy driving a 4 inch spike into a piece of lumber." No editorial comments will be made about the quality of his endeavours. On the other hand, if that scenario describes you or if you are equally soothed after a tough day by arranging a bouquet of flowers, then the benefits of an enjoyable hobby have significant positive results in coping.

Other hobbies are more interactive with people and those situations provide the same relaxing pluses, while coincidentally putting you in contact with people who could potentially assist you in your networking efforts.

In a similar vein, many of you have been so preoccupied with work that you have not had the chance to give anything more than dollars to charities and community projects. A renewed involvement in those activities can offer you a true sense of accomplishment while repaying obligations with time instead of money. Like hobbies, your active participation can also put you in touch with people who might be able to aid you in your job search.

Taking that thought a step further, in these days of major unemployment, more and more self-help groups are springing up. Several ad hoc associations are being formed to facilitate the sharing of ideas about how to tackle the job market. A quick perusal of your local Saturday or Sunday paper will likely put you in contact with these organizations. And the added bonus is they are there to help you and you are able to repay the other participants by sharing your ideas, suggestions and experiences.

Coping is not something which just happens. You need to be pro-active and alert to those activities which will genuinely help you through some of the difficult times which you are bound to encounter during your job search.

Routine

Most of us thrive on structure. It is the rare ex-management person who can function in a Bohemian lifestyle, particularly after years of being enslaved to schedules, deadlines and just plain routine. It is not in our nature to move from almost total structure to no framework whatsoever.

That is not to suggest you need to arise at precisely the same hour you did when you were going to work. Conversely, sleeping in until 9:00 A.M. every morning is not advocated either.

Take advantage of the temporary freedom offered by your time away from work but develop and adhere to a schedule which is good for you, your family and your job search. Make some alterations which force you to do things and get out. Just as an example, if you have always had the morning paper delivered, cancel the subscription and religiously start every morning off by walking to the corner store to pick up the publication. And how about all those veiled threats to start jogging again - lack of time can hardly be an excuse now. Jog for the morning paper!

As you advance into your job search, you will soon find that establishing or re-establishing a routine becomes even more critical. You will need a regiment to allow time for business reading, correspondence, research, meetings and yes, the general administration and organization required for your latest personal project - commonly know as the job search.

Remember a much earlier comment about establishing a set number of hours to be allocated to your job search? To achieve those goals you need a routine. Frittering away time in front of the television, by the pool or in the backyard will not advance your endeavours.

Educational Enhancement

Later in this book we will review your self-enhancement inventory but the section on coping seemed an ideal place to broach the issue of educational expansion. Much of the coping process depends upon purposeful activity which builds and maintains your self-confidence levels - those things that keep you up!

To many of us, there are two major reasons for expanding our education. One is because we have to and the other is because we want to. The most frequently used excuse for not pursuing educational enhancement is due to a supposed lack of time. That is not to suggest you can cram in a Ph.D. before you return to work but consider some or one of the following:

-        starting at least one of the courses required to complete your unfinished degree

-        finalizing one course relating to your chosen profession or selected field of endeavour

-        enrolling in stand-alone courses like business writing or presentation skills

-        upgrading or beginning some form of computer training

Let me touch on the latter item for a moment. There are some major myths about the computer fluency of the management work force. Corporate North America has realized the value of the computer and during the past decade these magic marvels have appeared on virtually every desk.

But are people using them to the optimum, if at all? Can we assume you have learned about computers simply by osmosis, due to their close proximity to you in your office? No! Granted, if a computer has been imposed upon you for internal communications through an Electronic Mail System, many managers will have mastered the key board - not always in the most proficient fashion. On/off switches have been located and there is a reasonable chance you can convert what is on the "little TV screen" into hard copy through the printer.

But what do you really know about computers?

Before being buried in an avalanche of letters and post cards from all the computer virtuosos and proficient computer users, it is readily acknowledged that a large portion of the management ranks can claim a sound level of knowledge about the computer. However, if you are among the 20 or 25 percent that have not taken the time to master at least a word processing package and perhaps one or two other basic applications, you need to take action now!

If you are still clinging to the fading hope that computers are a passing fad or that Corporate North America will soon awake and reinstate all the secretarial positions which have disappeared in the last 10 years, you truly are living in a world of your own. Even if you see yourself only working for another 5 years, you will still need some basic understanding of computers.

Courses in primary applications are inexpensive and if you are ill at ease about your lack of skill, remember this. Do you want to be a little uncomfortable in a class filled with equally un-proficient students or do you want to be totally embarrassed when you are in a work situation with your new employer?

Whatever you decide to do in terms of educational enhancement, expanding your horizons through learning will help you cope. You will feel a sense of pride and accomplishment. In many cases, you will be positioned to do your next job more effectively.

"Think Positive"

When researching this book, a number of people volunteered their opinions about various coping mechanisms which they had found most useful while in the job search mode. The main items have been covered, except for positive thinking. Most believed it was a factor but let's face it, a suggestion like "Think Positive" sounds a tad self-serving. At least it did until a once unemployed executive rendered some thoughts on the subject. As usual, KISS came into play again.

The philosophy starts with an assumption that there are two types of people in the world - those who constantly think positively and those who do not. Now just a minute, that can't be right, can it? Take a minute and jot down the names of ten people you know quite well, mixing in both personal friends and business associates. Place your name in the last position. Now ask yourself if you view them as a positive thinker or not. It is amazing how easy it is to categorize the people. How did you rate yourself?

The previously mentioned "scholar" who put forth this theorem, went on to say is was not necessary to address the issue of positive thinking for those who, by some quirk of nature, already fit in that category. However, for those who are in the other grouping, how do you go about attaining and maintaining a positive attitude?

One of the first and most simplistic means of doing this is to actually force yourself to frequently reflect on the beneficial impact of thinking positively. You and your family can have some fun with this one but let me give you a few examples:

1.   One individual who was extremely well organized in her job search had her networking dossier neatly filed in a large three ring binder which she referred to constantly. Taped to the front cover were two words in bold print "THINK POSITIVE".

2.   Another job seeker who happened to love his coffee, had an equally good way to remind himself. A business card, folded in half to form a mini tent card was perched atop the coffee maker at home, professing the same message. His comment was "I know I am going to be reminded to be positive at least 12 times a day."

3.   One of the more technical types who ran much of his job search campaign via his computer had built in a daily hot list item which beeped and flashed "THINK POSITIVE" each morning when he switched on the computer.

4.   Still another person and her spouse approached things a little differently by setting aside a few minutes around the dinner hour to each recount the positive things which had transpired during the day. What a great way for a job seeker to update a spouse on the events of the day. Coincidentally, the other partner had an opportunity to reflect on and share positive experiences as well. In this instance, the couple was coping through communication and by thinking positively.

By now, all the naturally positive thinkers will be nodding in full agreement about these seemingly insignificant ways to keep yourself motivated and positive. Those in the other category might be a little less convinced but the power of positive thinking can be an important ally. Give it a try and encourage yourself to make a genuine effort to actively include positive thinking in your daily routine.

Setting Achievable Goals

It would seem evident the job seeker should not encounter much difficulty in setting a goal. Find a job! Unfortunately, that well meaning goal can be self-defeating in terms of day-to-day coping.

Securing new employment is clearly an ultimate objective but exasperation can easily set in if you do not specifically set mini objectives throughout the course of your job search. To truly establish achievable goals, you must be in a position to control whether or not those self-imposed expectations can be met.

Stating you are going to be re-employed in four months is an admirable target but you do not have total control over the eventual outcome. On the other hand, laying out time frames for the completion of certain phases of your job search campaign are things you can personally drive and influence.

It is always wise to set challenging goals, but to assist yourself in coping, make certain they are within your own control, realistic and achievable.

The ways and means of coping are as different as people themselves. This chapter has offered up some basic ideas for your consideration but in the end, you must seek out and discover those activities which not only help you on a personal level but also aid you in advancing through your job search. Whatever you decide upon, you will be taking another step toward charting the direction of your own future.

Chapter 5

FOCUS ON THE FUTURE

Much of what has been covered in the preceding chapters has allowed you to reach a threshold where you can actually begin to look forward and start to re-plan your future. But before tackling the proper way to focus on the future, let me share with you one of the most common comments made by the recently unemployed. The remark goes something like this:

> "All I need is a little help updating my resume and then I'll be ready to tackle the market."

Wrong! Leaping forward to the preparation of a resume is akin to buying a map without first deciding where you want to go. The next most common piece of dialogue from the new job seeker can best be generalized by a statement such as:

> "I didn't mind my last position, I always did well in that field and I guess I should look for something in a similar line because that is basically all I have done in the past 10 years. Maybe my next employer will appreciate my talents more."

There may be some validity to many parts of the forgoing statement but stop and think for a moment. If your previous employer abolished your position, might this not suggest that other companies in like industries are doing the exact same thing! That is not to suggest you necessarily need to totally change the direction of your career but it does warrant some consideration and planning before deciding upon your future goals. Presumably, you do not want to be forced into another job search five years down the road.

At this juncture, you and perhaps your family need to start gathering and evaluating information. It is not as straight forward as deciding upon the type of job you want to find. Arriving at the right answer is not as simple as solving an elementary mathematical problem where you methodically arrive at a number of sub answers before coming up with the final solution.

As you begin to formulate a first draft career objective, you will need to investigate and assess several major components which can best be grouped under the following headings:

-        Personal / Family Objectives
-        Accomplishments
-        Self-Enhancement Inventory
-        Past Work Performance
-        Behavioral Assessment

Before looking at each of the above in greater detail, let me stress why this particular portion of the job search is often done poorly. Some of you are already checking the index to see where the resume writing chapter begins. At least take the time to read the balance of this chapter. Then you can decide if your job search should be solidly anchored on a well-formulated career objective or simply on a slick, professional looking resume.

For those of you who genuinely intend to work through this chapter, be forewarned! It is not necessarily an easy exercise and it does require time. Similarly, you need to be brutally honest, open minded and reflective.

Personal / Family Objectives

How often have you or someone you know said:

"If only I could get out of this rat race!"

"If I had it to do all over again, I would..."

"I'm sick of working in the concrete jungle."

"I really need to spend more time with the family."

"Money is important but..."

"Wouldn't it be great to really enjoy work again?"

Sound familiar? At one time or another, we have all voiced these views. For some, these types of comments are born from temporary exasperation but for others, these concerns have genuine meaning. If you are starting fresh, now is the time to truthfully investigate what you and your family ideally want.

At the end of the day, most of us will make some concessions and compromises but now is not the time to concede without carefully thinking through a variety of life and work situations. In an effort to get the imaginative juices flowing, sit down with your spouse and honestly answer the following questions:

- · Where would we live if we could choose virtually any community?

- What type of living accommodation would be considered ideal?

- And if the ideal accommodations are currently influenced by family situations, like children at home, when might this change?

- Would we both have to work or for that matter, would we both need to work?

- Ideally, what is the maximum distance or travel time between your home and work?

- Would we care if the work involved travel and what maximum tolerance levels would be acceptable in terms of duration and frequency?

- What does my new work environment look like? Is it in a downtown office tower, an industrial park, a shopping mall or do I care?

- What would we be willing to give up, if anything, if we could live and work exactly where we wanted?

- If there are children involved, how would such changes impact on them?

The purpose of answering these questions and openly discussing or reviewing other spin-off issues, is not necessarily to encourage you to pack your bags and become seashell sellers on the beaches of a forgotten tropical paradise. On the other hand, you may come to some conclusions which warrant immediate action or further consideration in the future.

You have also begun to build certain preference parameters regarding potential work locations and environments. Bear in mind, these are preferences but if you are being forced to make a change anyway, does it not make infinite sense to at least thoroughly investigate job options within the ideal parameters?

Perhaps the most sensitive issue to deal with and discuss candidly is money. Whether you like it or not, corporate life instills the thought that more is always better. A promotion a year, a more palatial office, better perks, bigger salaries, enhanced incentive programs, more prestigious titles and the like, have all become hallmarks of business and career success.

But are all those trappings truly important or have you and your family just got caught up on the merry-go-round? One of the most difficult decisions to make is to step back and then decide what you really want. The question you need to answer is "What do I want?" and not "What do my friends and associates think I have to have?" Only you and your family can determine to what degree ego and material niceties will play in how you want to fulfill your future personal and career goals.

As noted earlier, future focusing is not necessarily a step-by-step formula. The intent of this chapter is to cause you to consider a number of issues which collectively will influence your ultimate choice of a career objective. So temporarily put your thoughts about personal and family objectives on hold and we will move on to a first look at your past accomplishments.

Accomplishments

Almost every self help process talks about the importance of analyzing your past accomplishments. Quite legitimately, such exercises help you zero-in on those areas where you believe you have excelled and where you have enjoyed the rewards of a job well done. Properly completed, a thorough review of your accomplishments will also allow you to extract information which can highlight quantifiable success examples for your resume.

The reason most people skip over this step in future focusing is because they are convinced they can think of enough accomplishments to put into their resume. In fact, that output really only represents about 25% of the value derived from the process. What you are attempting to gain is some insight about what situations you thrive in and enjoy. By normal extension, these examples will reflect your saleable strengths. In short, where you function with the greatest degree of comfort, panache and effectiveness.

Digressing for a moment, you might also discover the self-awareness you gain will begin to explain why you did not like certain aspects of previous positions and assignments. Note: do not confuse liking a task with whether or not you were able to get the job done or even done in a very proficient manner.

What is an accomplishment? Here are **three** broad guidelines which you will want to keep in mind as you read and work through the balance of this section. An accomplishment should be something:

1.   You have done well and you view the results with a true sense of pride.

2.   You have enjoyed from start to finish, ignoring minor irritants along the way.

3.   You can readily explain and illustrate the positive results.

Do not make the mistake of only looking for the "big picture" accomplishments. You may want to reflect on past monthly or even daily routines to determine if there were smaller components of your work which provided you with a sense of pride. Just as an example, you may have effectively headed up a twenty person accounting department for the past five years but the component of the job which you most enjoyed was personally preparing and presenting the monthly financial results to the executive committee.

You may not have truly enjoyed running the department on a day to day basis but you did look forward to compiling the monthly reports with great precision and detailing the outcome to others.

Again, do not limit your thinking to the past few years. Draw on your full range of life experiences right from your high school days through to the present time. This is a self-assessment process and no one is going to know if you still look back on your summer camp counselling work as one of the most meaningful and rewarding times in your entire life. Similarly, accomplishments can relate to situations outside the realm of work. If you thoroughly enjoyed planning, designing and renovating your personal residence, then that becomes a significant accomplishment.

A word of caution. Most people can not sit down and list eight accomplishments in a half hour. There are no rewards for speed when it comes to listing and analyzing your own accomplishments. Start the list and keep coming back to it. You might want to get some outside input from your spouse or a close friend. Others can often trigger your memory. Take your time and develop a solid list of accomplishments that you feel good about.

Once you have a line on your accomplishments, sit down and work through a review of each, using the following general format. The questions you are going to give some thought to are not being raised to simply fill in a nice looking form.

SELF ASSESSING YOUR ACCOMPLISHMENTS

-       Briefly describe the accomplishment.

-       When did it take place and where?

- Where were you working or what were you doing?

- What was the issue you were dealing with and how did it lead to a significant accomplishment?

- Describe all the steps you took which lead to the successful completion of the undertaking.

- If you had a boss at the time, describe that person and how they managed.

- If subordinates were involved, describe them and note how many were involved.

As suggested earlier, what you are attempting to do is to get a firm handle on what you perceive to be your accomplishments and in what situations these occurred. It is for this reason the questions are posed and when you have completed all eight scenarios, you will see some trends emerging. Here are a few typical examples:

- Accomplishments may fit within specific time frames, suggesting your work or residency may have been an influencing factor.

- Significant accomplishments may be seen to coincide with having a particular type of boss, such as the one who offered a great deal of autonomy.

- You might discover you enjoyed situations where you started with a lackluster group of people and you ultimately developed them into a team.

- Conversely, you might see more evidence of accomplishments when you were directing a team of highly qualified professionals who needed little or no direction.

- Other trends might suggest an affinity to project type work where you were given a specific objective, you went in, got it done and then moved on to another challenge.

- On other occasions, you might conclude you enjoy the security of a methodical and repetitive set of tasks, or in other words, a more structured work environment.

Reviewing past accomplishments is extremely important in terms of the overall job search process. As you have no doubt found, to complete a comprehensive review takes a good deal of effort, honesty and reflection. The above examples are intended to give you a sense of what some people have gleaned from evaluating their own accomplishments.

To give you a hand in distilling the information and in arriving at more specific conclusions, re-read the eight pieces of paper you have in front of you. Then answer the following questions. Again, this exercise may be easier if you have the help of your spouse or a close friend.

WHAT HAVE I LEARNED?

- Do I like working with others?

- If I do, do I like being a participative team player or do I prefer to lead / direct subordinates?

- What type of boss do I like working for?

- Do I function better when there is only one boss or am I at ease when I have several masters?

- Am I a high risk taker or do I prefer to have my authority boundaries carefully delineated?

-       Is the size of my employer important or does it really matter?

-       Am I looking for significant promotional opportunities in the next five years?

-       When would I like to retire and would I prefer to remain with my next employer until I retire?

-       Do I really enjoy managing others and if I have subordinates, what type of people are they?

-       How important is salary?

-       What type of physical environment do I like and where is it in relationship to my residence?

-       What degree of independence am I seeking in a work situation?

-       Are hours important and if so, what are the outer or upper limits? What are my limitations involving business travel?

-       What non-base salary considerations might be important? Consider such items as bonus systems, leased vehicles and benefits.

Having answered these questions, you have now begun to formulate a pool of information which will aid you in clearly enunciating your career objective(s). As you move through the other phases of focusing for the future, periodically come back to the answers you have recorded in the "What Have I Learned?" questionnaire. These responses are not cast in concrete and in fact, you should make some modifications as you learn even more about yourself and what you want to do.

Self-Enhancement Inventory

For most of us, the difficulty of the next exercise is directly related to the amount of time we have spent in the work force - ergo, it requires a good memory!

People seldom take stock of the things they have done to enhance themselves. What better time to do so than when you are headed into situations where potential employers are going to ask pointed questions about your education, skills, personal development goals and interests.

Just to get started, take a blank sheet of paper and turn the clock back to your last year of high-school. List down every course you can remember taking that year. Do not be too concerned about the ones you can not recall. Such memory lapses are usually a reasonable commentary on the worth or degree of interest you had in those classes.

From there, move into your university days and do the same thing, but do not limit yourself to the last year. Then, employer by employer, list down every organized learning opportunity which you were given, excluding day to day or on-the-job learning experiences. The list should include in-house training courses, outside seminars, conventions, symposiums, conferences and literally any other situation where you have had an opportunity to formally enhance yourself.

Now, think back on any courses, home study scenarios or continuing education programs which you have taken on your own. Do not forget to record those which you took for pure pleasure, whether they were:

-       "Basket Weaving"
-       "How to Wire the Basement"
-       "Introduction to Computers"

-     "Interior Design Made Easy"
-     "Helping the Environment Through Recycling"

Backtrack to the top of the list and rate each item with one of three words - GREAT, OK or HO-HUM. These ratings should be based purely on enjoyment and not how well you scored, if indeed marks were involved. Granted, this is not the most sophisticated rating system but the list will quickly illustrate where you have had an opportunity to enhance yourself and what areas you naturally gravitated toward in terms of enjoyment.

Not long ago, a friend of mine who had previously been in the systems side of business went through this same exercise. He had always scored in the upper ranges of any academic endeavour within the systems field but he was perplexed by his own honest answers. He had rated most of the hard core systems courses as "OK" but whenever he was exposed to marketing related learning experiences, his own ratings shot up to the "Great" category.

You may not be surprised to learn that after holding several successful positions in systems administration, this individual re-focused his career toward sales within a systems environment. His decision was not driven solely by the foregoing exercise but when combining this information with the other conclusions he arrived at in focusing for the future, he was able to clearly see what direction would be most enjoyable and would make the most sense.

You might also stumble upon some harsh realities which you may not want to face. Most notably, you may discover you have not had an opportunity or you *have not taken the opportunity* to enhance yourself since you finished your formal education. The excuses or explanations for this set of circumstances will range from legitimate to feeble and whatever the reason, you can not go back to capitalize on lost opportunities. But what you can do is make some informed decisions about what you must accomplish in the future and formulate a specific plan of attack.

And start NOW! You will recall the concerns mentioned before about the need for managers to bone up on basic computer skills. If you fall in that category, put this book down now, go to your phone book and then make 5 calls to gather information about computer courses. Then set yourself a goal of signing up for one of those classes within the next week.

If you want to be pragmatic about self-enhancement, ask yourself or ask any management person what response they like to hear when posing the age old interviewing question - "Tell me a little bit about how you keep current on the rapid changes which are occurring in our field and can you give me some specific past examples of how you have accomplished this?"

The reply must be honest but you can go a long way to setting an interviewer's mind at ease if you can recount your future game plan, including a list of committed actions which are already underway.

For those of you who may ultimately lean toward different career directions, take the time to specifically research what ongoing self-enhancement is preferable, expected or required in your potential new field. How many of you have known someone who wanted to get into real estate or some other venture, only to have a change of heart when they discovered there was a huge time commitment needed to earn the necessary regulatory credentials.

Just as the expression implies, self-enhancement is truly dependent upon you, and your future successful employment will be tied in some fashion to your degree of commitment to expanding your personal and professional horizons.

Review of Past Performance

Performance reviews - the annual or even more frequent undertaking which we all dread! Actually, dread might be too strong but few of us relished completing reports on subordinates. Similarly, we did not like being placed under the performance microscope, even if we were confident the outcome would be fully satisfactory or even better.

Based on twenty five years in corporate life and after seeing the long parade of performance evaluation methodologies, ranging from the one page tick-sheet to the volumes required for target oriented performance reviews, the following conclusions are inevitable:

1.   Few people like doing performance reviews.

2.   Even fewer people take the necessary time to complete performance reviews properly.

3.   Raters most often err on the side of the employee to avoid confrontation.

So you might well ask why this issue should even be broached. Why would reviewing your own past performance be a means of assisting you in arriving at a future focus? The answer rests in another truism which is quickly discovered by those who have reviewed or compiled literally thousands of performance evaluations.

The key word to remember is TREND. If you are one of those methodical people who has kept every evaluation ever done on you, go to your filing cabinet in the basement and pull them all out. If you do not fall in the compulsive pack-rat category, you should consider asking your most recent employer for copies of your last four or five reviews.

As an aside, if you have not signed off on your settlement, you could encounter some resistance to the latter request as there may be a concern you are searching for ammunition to launch a legal action. Circumstances will vary from company to company, but if you explain you want the information to conduct some self-assessment, preparatory to your job search, the data will likely be forthcoming.

Now, quickly read through the reports, simply to get yourself in the right frame of mind. It will assist you in recalling some of the major events in your work history. Then go through every report you have and critically record the most positive comment or rating and the least positive.

Generally speaking, you will find few surprises in the plus column. But what you discover on the other side of the ledger may cause you to re-read some of the evaluations in an attempt to disprove the trend which has emerged.

In all likelihood, you will find consistencies showing through and while they might not be classified as true weaknesses, they are certainly areas where you do not naturally excel. Indeed, many of these items can be lumped under the heading of "Things I Can Do But I Don't Like Doing" and you should be honest about these issues.

So what is the purpose of dredging up this supposed enlightening information? First, it is important to recognize and acknowledge your own soft spots and second, you may need to develop a game plan to deal with these issues in the future.

Clearly, you will want to weigh these factors as you begin to focus on future job objectives. It does not take a rocket scientist to conclude you should not be seeking positions which have components weighted heavily toward areas which do not align with your natural abilities, interests and resultant strengths.

On the other hand, you may come to the realization that you need to take some affirmative or corrective action to improve in certain areas. For example, take time management. Perhaps no one has ever said you are a terrible manager of time but if innocent phrases like some of the following have been sprinkled through your last five reviews, you may want to do some soul searching.

-       occasionally misses deadlines....
-       promptness could be improved at times....
-       can leave assignments to the last minute....
-       could plan more effectively for contingencies....

Consider equally the "less positive" and the "positive" aspects. You are much more apt to already know and acknowledge the pluses but taking the time to capture and review them will assist you in preparing a progressive resume.

By critically reviewing the "less positive" items, you will be in a much better position to set some career objectives which might avoid work situations demanding a significant degree of concentration on areas where you are not naturally strong.

Before moving to the next section, return to your "What Have I Learned?" list and make any necessary additions, deletions and changes. By now you should be getting a feel for your areas of interest. Those will become more important as you move toward actually setting a firm career objective.

Behavioral Assessment

Up to this point, we have concentrated on future focusing which has really been accomplished through self-assessment. In other words, you taking the time to critically reflect on historical events and related data. Coincidentally, you have used this information to begin to develop a meaningful future focus which is realistic, attainable and in sync with a potential career direction and life style you and your family would enjoy.

The one item which most unassisted job seekers (those not supported by re-employment counselling firms) do not investigate is some form of behavioral evaluation which can be combined with a candid self-assessment. One reason for not pursuing this important step is because most people do not know where to find this type of support. The second reason is that everyone, deep down, is somewhat skeptical about the perceived mysteries associated with psychological evaluations. The latter statement is in no way intended to discredit psychologists or industrial psychologists. Perhaps we have all spent too much time watching re-runs of early Bob Newhart sitcoms.

The third and forth reasons relate to cost and understandability. There are a vast array of assessment vehicles on the market but few can be easily self-interpreted. And the expense associated with having an assessment prepared, can often be quite prohibitive if you are footing your own bill.

In an effort to minimize all of these objections, arrangements have been made with Thomas International Management Systems Inc. to offer you the means to acquire a common sense and valuable behavioral assessment. You can choose to move forward to your objective setting phase without this component but do take a moment to read the example which typifies the output you could receive (See Appendix - Graphics & Forms # 6 for more details).

Alternatively, you can seek out other assessment vehicles or perhaps you already have some reasonably current data from assessments which were completed by a former employer.

Assessments must not be acted upon in isolation. It is critical to understand that any form of professional assessment is simply another tool to assist you in reaching an informed decision about a proper career direction.

As you conclude the work associated with this chapter, the elements of your future focus should be crystallizing. Armed with that information you will be prepared to move forward to crafting a specific career objective and the resume which will flow from all your previous preparation.

Chapter 6

DEFINING YOUR
CAREER OBJECTIVES

What am I good at? What do I like doing? What have I learned
about myself? Where do I head? What do I specifically want to
do? How do I capture my objective in words?

This is perhaps the most difficult chapter to write because giving
directions about defining a career objective seems to immediately
call for a two way dialogue. Failing that, the best place to start is
to analyze just what is a career objective. In the simplest of terms,
it is what you want to do. When thinking about a career objective,
there is a natural inclination to focus on the objective statement
which introduces many of today's resumes. That statement, almost
a personal mission statement if you will, is extremely important
because it defines / describes:

-       What you want to do and how you will go about doing it.

-       Where you want to work (the environment, the industry or
        the type of employer).

What many people fail to realize is the fact these words on a page can not be hollow phrases, strung together solely to capture the interest of someone reading your resume. Take a moment and think back to the company mission statements you have been exposed to in the past. You do not have to recall the exact sentences but consider whether or not the words etched on those prominently displayed plaques were truly the underlying philosophy which guided the company on a day-to-day basis. In short, were the words a true depiction of the actions?

You will likely recall more situations where the words and the actions did not seem to coincide. In other instances you will remember companies where "what they said" was "what they did" and they were true to their stated corporate direction. Your career objective statement must be a true and meaningful recounting of your intentions.

During the course of your job search, you will be asked on countless occasions to explain your goals. It is one thing to articulate your objective in words but it is even more important to be able to back those words up with genuine expressions of your value, your ability to contribute and your personal commitment.

As you have read and worked through some of the preceding chapters, you will have begun to formulate some personal impressions about yourself. In some cases, you will have experienced a sense of confirmation and in other scenarios, you may have been startled by your conclusions.

The balance of this chapter will assist you in taking what you have learned, to concentrate that information into a crisp career objective - one which you can support not only with words but also with actions. At this point, you likely have too much data and you will need to begin the process of editing the mountains of paper and thoughts you have accumulated.

"Play to your strengths!" That expression is universally applicable, whether you are a professional athlete, an entertainer, a politician, a senior executive, a secretary, a manager or anyone in between. And just where do you discover your strengths? In your accomplishments! Your past accomplishments will highlight your true strengths, where there is a natural fusion between your interests and your skills/abilities.

Remember, if you have an ability but no interest, there is no strength. If you have an interest but no ability, there is no strength. If you have an interest *and* an ability, you have honed in on a real strength.

Your challenge is to determine and identify those strengths which are unique to you. Go back to your accomplishments and re-read your notes. Then go through them a second time but on this occasion, bear in mind the following list. The list is not exhaustive but it will give you a starting point. Circle those words which most apply to you when you ask yourself the important question: " Do I have a true ability to ..." If you come across one of your abilities which is not recorded, add it to the list.

Administer	Analyze	Arbitrate
Build	Challenge	Control
Create	Direct	Empathize
Explore	Imagine	Innovate
Install	Interpret	Lead
Maintain	Observe	Operate
Organize	Perform	Persuade
Plan	Present	Procure
Serve	Solve	Strategize
Sympathize	Synthesize	Systematize
Visualize	Others....	

Recalling all the self-assessment work you have completed, review the circled abilities and make notations where you have a keen interest. Remember, an interest should not include areas where you simply have a casual or passing feeling of interest. Key in on those items where you have a real passion and sense of enjoyment. The combination of an interest and an ability yield notable personal strengths.

You have now roughly identified your true areas of strength. Carefully analyze these and choose three or four that rank highest in your mind. If you are encountering difficulty, seek some outside input from your spouse, a close friend or an old mentor. This is not a ten minute exercise. Your choices and decisions will influence your entire job search and in the very near future, you will be translating your strengths into words and committed actions.

The next critical step is to take your strengths and equate those to industries where your identified talents might be used. Be forewarned, it is extremely easy to fall into the trap of immediately returning to your previous career, industry or profession.

At this juncture, a little brainstorming with yourself or others can be very beneficial to broaden the horizons of your thinking and to identify possible different work scenarios where your strengths have transferability. In the vast majority of cases, you will discover your strengths easily transcend industry or business boundaries.

Now comes the hard part, not to suggest all the previous work has not been taxing! Based on your strengths and the industry or business sectors which appeal to you, you must now craft an objective statement. Let's start by reviewing some objective statements which would be classified as poor or at best, very average.

"To achieve a position where I can put my marketing experience to use in a progressive company."

"To assume a Vice President level job where I can utilize my past banking exposure to the greatest degree with a financial services company."

"To utilize my varied background in systems project management within a company which is moving ahead quickly in developing new technology."

"To assume a General Managers position in a forward thinking company where my broad management skills can be put to the fullest use possible."

These examples use some of the proper phrases but all of them are too vague. They center on what the writer wants and they do not accent the strengths of the individual. In an effort to assist you in developing and refining your objective statements, carefully review and analyze the following. These statements clearly outline who you are, what you have to offer and in what type of environment you want to contribute your talents.

"To secure a challenging position where my marketing talents and progressive experience can be optimized in a leading edge national organization."

"To assume a senior level position which will allow a dynamic financial services organization to capitalize on my diverse banking background."

"To take a lead role in a project management capacity within a rapidly developing multinational organization where technological change is seen as a catalyst in strategic planning and tactical implementation."

"To assume a General Management position where my proven and wide ranging management abilities can lead a diverse group of employees in achieving and exceeding aggressive manufacturing targets for a regionally based corporation."

Creating your own objective statement is not a task to be taken lightly and the final version is not apt to be achieved on the first attempt. When you have finalized your personal "Mission Statement" it should be a natural extension of who you are, what you excel in and where you want to be.

You will know when you have struck on the right words when you can say with confidence:

> "This is me, this is what I am good at and this is what I want to be!"

If you have written a sound career objective, you will find your resume will flow easily and will totally support the career direction you have chosen for yourself. Sit back and admire your objective with pride, you have earned it!

Chapter 7

CRAFTING YOUR RESUME

So, what is the big deal about writing a resume? Just take a few personal bits of information, add company names and dates, extract a couple of key responsibilities from old position descriptions, record one or two previous great sounding titles, toss in a few well-chosen hobbies and finish up with two or three references. Done!

If that is your recipe for a resume, the results will be about as appetizing and as effective as many half-baked ideas. Most of you are anxious to hit the job search trail but this is not time to take short cuts. Your resume should be a professional depiction of who you are, where you have been, what you have done and above all else, what you are capable of accomplishing or contributing to a new employer. In other words: here is who I am, this is what I have to offer and this is what sets me apart from others.

In the event your previous employment placed you in contact with a variety of incoming resumes, take a moment and think back on what you did not like to see. For those of you who did not have to endure the agony of reviewing and reading poor resumes, here are some hints about what not to do:

-   Don't be slick, glittery or cute. A good recruiter or interviewer will see through a superficial resume in minutes.

-   Don't recount your entire life and work history in minute detail. By the very virtue of the word, a resume implies a brief overview.

-   Don't embellish the truth. There is a vast difference between positioning yourself positively and out and out deception. Go with your strengths, not fiction.

-   Don't assume the content alone is going to be good enough to sell you.

Before progressing to some of the fundamentals of good resume writing, there are a few myths to be dispelled and some facts to remember:

-   Resumes alone do not secure jobs.

-   Poor resumes can disqualify you before you have a chance to present yourself.

-   Good resumes can enhance your opportunities to showcase your wares in person.

All of that to say, toiling over a well written resume is a very important part of your job search. But remember, it is only one component in the entire process. You will be quickly disillusioned if you place too much emphasis or faith in your resume alone. This chapter is not intended to teach you how to write the perfect resume but rather, it will offer some background information to assist you in developing a resume which will complement and strengthen your overall job search strategy.

In the previous chapter, we addressed the issue of establishing a concise objective. Indeed, much of the first part of this book has been devoted to assisting you in determining a focus, bearing in mind your personal preferences and the career path you wish to pursue. Part of the rationale for this labourious procedure was to help you in preparing for the completion of a well crafted resume. One which states what you want and supports that goal with tangible evidence.

All too often, people without a proper focus discover they are constantly changing and reworking their resumes. If you find this is happening to you, there is a strong probability you have not focused on your true career objective and you should consider retracing your steps.

Once you have completed your resumes, there should be no need to tinker with the format or the content, unless you have a major shift in career direction. Your covering letters and personal discussions should be the venues to accent any nuances required to progress your job search with potential employers.

Resume Types

Resumes fall into two main categories - functional and chronological. For the uninitiated resume writer, this choice can appear to be yet another hurdle to vault. Actually, the selection process is not an issue because you should do both. Granted, one will likely be used 80% of the time but there is nothing more exasperating than being confronted with an urgent situation where the alternate type of resume would be more appropriate.

If you are taking the time to develop a first class resume, you might just as well expend a little more energy and prepare both formats. In fact, after you have laboured over the format which will be used most frequently, you will discover the second resume will come together quite quickly.

Just to be clear, there are some valid reasons or situations which may influence the use of either a functional or chronological resume. If you intend to remain in a field which closely aligns with your previous career path a chronological resume could be the most appropriate choice, particularly if it is evident from the resume that you have assumed increasingly more responsible positions over the years.

 As a side note, those who have climbed the corporate ladder with a single employer may want to consider a functional resume to highlight key abilities and initially down play exposure to only one employer. Functional resumes tend to be more useful in situations where you are considering a career change and again, you want to accent key abilities, responsibilities and resultant accomplishments.

Similarly, if it could be perceived you have been hopping from job to job, the functional resume allows you to focus on the variety of experiences you have acquired, versus a long list of previous employers. That is not to suggest you should attempt to hide the fact you have had several employers but you always want to lead with your positives. In some career streams which are more project based, having a number of employers is not uncommon and often times expected.

When you have basically completed the final draft of both resumes, ask for some candid input from a few people who you trust and respect. If your chosen career direction includes venturing into new arenas, you might want to ask for some feedback during your initial networking meetings to garner impressions from those who are more conversant with an industry sector which may be somewhat foreign to you.

Resume Standards

For both formats, there are some basic rules or accepted practices which deserve comment and your careful consideration. If you recall the second paragraph in this chapter, you want your resume to outline and convey the following information:

- Here is who I am.
- This is what I have to offer.
- This is what sets me apart from others.

In essence, you are taking a great deal of data and distilling or recapping it into an advertising piece which is an honest representation. The effectiveness of your resume is not directly proportionate to the length. Indeed, the converse is closer to the truth and you should aim for a total of two pages or three at the absolute outside. Everyone thinks they are the exception to this guideline but a resume is intended to capture the highlights, not your entire life and work history. Additional background will be covered during the discussion and interview stages.

Over and above recapping pertinent data, a resume should be viewed as a high quality, professional advertisement. Do not overlook the need for truth in advertising! The content of the resume is a reflection of who you are and the manner of presentation should re-enforce those qualities.

As such, the presentation should be on superior quality paper and that theme should carry through to all your written communications. You will receive widely varying suggestions about the color of paper which is most effective but unless your chosen field dictates the need for something exotic, keep it simple and conservative.

Bright white, off white, light buff or light grey are all safe bets. Take some time before you decide and use the same paper for both your letters and your resumes. This route simplifies matters for you. Then go out and purchase 500 sheets of paper. Avoid buying "Resume Kits" as they are expensive and you will be forever trekking back to the stationery store for more.

If you decide to have your resume professionally reproduced, make certain the font is the same as, or complementary to, the font you will be using in your covering letters. For those of you who have access to a bubble jet or laser printer, it is likely just as easy to print your resumes on an "as needed" basis. Your cash flow may be a little tight but in the long run, now could be the time to invest three or four hundred dollars in an inexpensive bubble jet printer.

The Resume

As was the case with setting an objective, books have the disadvantage of being a one-sided dialogue. In an effort to assist you in preparing an effective resume, carefully read the following section.

Both functional and chronological resumes incorporate five major components:

> 1. Personal Data
> 2. Objective Statement
> 3. Key Qualifications
> 4. Professional Experience
> 5. Other Useful Data

The Resume - Personal Data & Objective Statement

Items one and two are straight forward although it is worthwhile to be very clear about your "Known As" if it differs from your full or usual name. The solution is as simple as bracketing your usual name, thereby avoiding any confusion during follow up calls and interviews.

Similarly, always record your telephone area code in the event a prospective employer's regional or head office is outside your local calling area. Completing section two is simply a matter of transcribing the final version of your personal objective statement.

The Resume - Key Qualifications

If the Objective Statement sets out what you want to do, the "Key Qualifications" section can best be described as what you can do most effectively. Occasionally you will see the expression "Significant Career Achievements" used to denote the same information. In essence the Key Qualifications highlight your most notable strengths. That said, you might find one or two of the recorded items accent your knowledge or previously demonstrated abilities and skills.

Just as an example, you may wish to note technical proficiencies relating to such things as computer skills, knowledge concerning very specific aspects of your profession or other pertinent data. These could encompass your understanding of new leading edge business concepts, perhaps special language capabilities or even exposure to work environments outside your own country.

Selecting your Key Qualifications is extremely important as readers of your resume naturally gravitate to this concise recap as it truly represents a precis within a precis. If you will, it becomes your "store front" advertising which draws the reader in, to more closely check out what you have to offer.

Taking the concept a step further, the presentation of the entire first page of your resume is critical in terms of conveying an initial and favourable impression. You will notice from each of the resume examples, the format and content of page one is always:

- Eye catching
- Clean and un-cluttered
- Precise and to the point
- Professionally presented

The Resume - Professional Experience

The "Professional Experience" section or the body of the resume usually presents the biggest writing challenge. As the title of this chapter suggests, a professional resume must be crafted if it is to suit you and your job search requirements.

The examples at the end of this chapter are supplied to give you a sense of what an effective resume should impart and look like. Each "Professional Experience" section has been designed to illustrate various proven approaches which outline how to record previous responsibilities and incorporate the positive results which you have generated. It is usually helpful to frequently refer back to the notes you have accumulated while preparing to write your Objective Statement.

Crafting your own resume takes time and it is highly unlikely you will complete the task in one sitting. The most accomplished resume writer will be the first to emphasize the importance of re-writing, editing and polishing your work. You could easily find this may take a week or two until you are fully satisfied with the final version.

If you are not comfortable with your own resume, take the time to research the host of other publications which specialize in addressing this important document.

The Resume - Other Useful Data

There are a wide variety of items which could be covered under the "Other Useful Data" category. The key word being useful. Common sense must apply to the amount of detail which is included in this section, otherwise it could literally take up a full page. The best rule of thumb is to carefully consider what elements of your personal background are of likely interest to the types of employers you are apt to be contacting.

The list of inclusions are mind boggling if you look at some of the suggested topics which can be contained in this section, such as: education, other courses, special awards, published articles, personal interests, community service, memberships, references and military service. To simplify matters, these and other sundry items can be grouped into three main categories:

1. Education
- Academic credentials / thesis / awards
- Professional enhancement studies
2. Personal
- Interests
- Memberships
- Community service
- Military service
- Published articles / books
3. References

The Resume - Other Useful Data - Education

In terms of the education section, your academic achievements should be listed in reverse chronological order, simply stating the degree attained, when and from what university or college. If you were the recipient of any noteworthy and relevant awards these can be noted, particularly if you graduated within the past 5 to 7 years.

It may be impractical to list all the professional enhancement studies you have completed but select those which are germane to your objective. Likewise, if you have written a thesis which is still considered timely and topical, it can best be inserted under the education section.

The Resume - Other Useful Data (Personal)

The personal section of the resume has shrunken considerably over the past ten years, in large measure due to legislative restrictions. What you choose to include should not be seen as "filler" but rather, information of substance. Being an avid sports enthusiast may have minimal applicability if you are seeking a position as a computer analyst but it may be more relevant if you are applying for a marketing job where sports are directly or indirectly linked to the position.

Caution should be exercised in listing memberships and community involvements. If you are inclined to include such items, they should be:

-       pertinent to positions of interest to you
-       non controversial
-       involvements of substance

Just to illustrate, being the coach of a little league softball team has relevance if you are applying for positions in a field which is sports-related or is closely tied to athletic activities. Recording your directorship on the board of a "Pro Life" or "Pro Choice" organization is of no consequence or benefit, unless your job search is specifically focused on one of these two avenues. Even then, it would have to be very closely related to the jobs in question. By the same token, references to political or religious affiliations are of no use, unless they directly relate to your search.

Being a United Way canvasser for two weeks a year at the office could be seen as an admirable undertaking but it is likely not worth noting. Conversely, being seconded for three months to chair a major portion of the local United Way Campaign is probably worthy of inclusion.

References to military service are not necessary unless this forms part of your professional history and then it should probably be recorded in the work experience section. On occasion, recording military reserve work may be appropriate if it has specific applicability to the positions which you are seeking.

If you have been published and the topics of your articles, books or professional papers relate to the type of work you are seeking, such publications should likely be interwoven into the accomplishments noted in the professional experience section. If the subject or topic is unrelated, you may decide to record a brief notation under the personal category.

Your resume is not intended to provide the reader with a sense of your personal life, habits, opinions and philosophies. Inserting too much personal trivia will raise more questions than can be adequately explained in any resume. You will have ample time in networking or interview situations to impart some personal information, when and where you can use it to your advantage in supporting and progressing you candidacy for a job.

The Resume - Other Useful Data (References)

The entire issue of references is highly overrated, at least in the initial phases of your job search. Listing three or four references on your resume is a waste of valuable space and you can be assured that no company will start the time consuming and expensive process of thoroughly checking references until you are at least on a short list of candidates for a position. Frankly, who in their right mind would record names of people who would supply a poor reference!

That is not to say you should not give considerable thought to who you will use as references when the appropriate time comes but for the purposes of a resume, it is quite sufficient to state references will be provided upon request.

Now that your resume has been completed in final form, you are ready to activate your actual job search campaign. The balance of this book will deal with preparing for that venture and executing a well-organized networking strategy.

Example Number One - Chronological

MS. DALE LEDGER

2010 Organize Road - Apt. #1002
Calgary, Alberta T2P 9R8

403-555-2002

OBJECTIVE

"To assume a senior level position which will allow a dynamic financial services organization to capitalize on my diverse banking background."

SIGNIFICANT CAREER ACHIEVEMENTS

- Achieved 12.4% ($150 million) growth in investment portfolio through development of a breakthrough strategy for area branches focused on: strong team effort, relationship building, timely responsiveness and customer satisfaction.

- Reduced staffing levels by 20% resulting in $1 million in expense savings, while increasing efficiency of operations, client satisfaction and sales volumes to achieve record net income growth of 50%.

- Obtained in excess of $10 million in new investment business through personal involvement in relationship development of major clients.

- Successfully led and directed an amalgamation project of two major full service branches with a combined staff of 150 and client base of 35,000 accounts. Orchestrated administration logistics, staffing considerations, ongoing sales effectiveness and client satisfaction.

- Developed the premiere sales team yielding an increase in RRSP sales over 3 years from $500,000 to over $7 million.

- Established and fostered open communications with the Corporate Lenders resulting in a 30% increase in their contribution to sales.

PROFESSIONAL EXPERIENCE - Financial Institution (1973-1993)

Branch Manager - Calgary, Alberta (1990-1994)

Effectively led a full service branch team with a complement of 95, consisting of a Corporate Business Unit, Retail Banking Centre and a Sales & Service Centre focusing on:

-       Market segmentation to identify prime potential opportunities together with the design and implementation of specific sales strategies.
-       Relationship building targeted at the highest potential segments through client profiling, needs identification and financial planning.
-       Human resource development consisting of skills assessment and enhancement, career path identification, developmental action planning and effective coaching.

District Manager (Central Region) - Brandon, Manitoba (1988-1989)

Successfully led a team of 35 branch managers focusing on:

-       Development and implementation of sales and marketing strategies resulting in continuous achievement of business plans, increasing profitability by 23% and expanded client base by 18% in two years.
-       Introduced effective risk management strategies, reducing non-performing loan dollar volumes by 13%.
-       Championed a quality customer service initiative resulting in a 30% reduction in customer complaints as qualified by: surveys, focus groups and client questionnaire responses.

Manager, Human Resources - Vancouver B.C. (1986-1987)

General management responsibility for the regional human resources function:

-       Development and implementation of succession planning programs concentrating on: identification of high potential employees, developmental action plans and career fast-tracking initiatives.
-       Preparation and control of the regional human resources financial plan, entailing: remuneration, staffing levels and training programs, resulting in consistent plan achievement.
-       Developed and introduced regional training programs leading to: increased levels of personnel development, skill enhancement, motivation and commitment.

PROFESSIONAL EXPERIENCE - Other Positions Held

Senior Manager, Head Office Retail Loan Division (1984-1985)

Manager, Regional Retail Loan Operations (1982-1983)

Inspector, International Audit and Control Division (1980-1981)

Senior Account Manager, Corporate Lending (1976-1979)

Account Manager, Commercial Lending (1974-1975)

Various developmental and administrative positions (1973)

EDUCATION

Bachelor of Arts, University of Calgary (1972)
Executive Development Program, Banff School of Management (1991)
Fellow - Institute of Canadian Bankers (1981)
Various internal leadership, marketing and human resource studies

PERSONAL

Member - Chamber of Commerce (1989 - Present)
Commercial Campaign Coordinator - Calgary United Way (1992)

REFERENCES

References available upon request.

Example Number Two - Functional

MS. DALE LEDGER

2010 Organize Road - Apt. #1002
Calgary, Alberta T2P 9R8

403-555-2002

OBJECTIVE

"To assume a senior level position which will allow a dynamic financial services organization to capitalize on my diverse banking background."

KEY QUALIFICATIONS

- Leader and people developer
- Innovative strategic thinker
- Tactical problem solver

- Profit oriented
- Client service focus
- Motivational communicator

PROFESSIONAL EXPERIENCE

Human Resource Management

- Developed and introduced regional training programs leading to: increased levels of personnel development, skill enhancement, motivation and commitment.
- Coached and directed a premiere sales team responsible for increasing RRSP sales over 3 years from $500,000 to over $7 million.
- Implemented succession planning programs concentrating on: identification of high potential employees, developmental action plans and career fast-tracking initiatives.
- Expanded human resource development plans to include: behavioral assessment, career path identification, and action directives.
- Prepared and controlled a regional human resources financial plan, entailing: remuneration, staffing levels and training programs, resulting in consistent plan achievement.

Marketing

- Developed and initiated sales and marketing strategies which resulted in continuous achievement of business plans, increasing profitability by 23% and expanded client base by 18% in two years.
- Conducted market segmentation studies to identify prime opportunities, followed by the design and implementation of sales strategies.
- Designed relationship building initiatives, targeted at the highest potential market segments through client profiling and needs identification.
- Championed a quality customer service initiative resulting in a 30% reduction in customer complaints as qualified by: surveys, focus groups and client questionnaire responses.

Management

- Assumed increasingly demanding positions culminating in the management of the most profitable full-service branch in southern Alberta, accomplishing:

  - A 12.4% ($150 million) growth in investment portfolio through development of a breakthrough strategy focused on: team effort, relationship building, responsiveness and customer satisfaction.
  - Fostered open communications with the Corporate Lenders resulting in a 30% increase in their contribution to consumer sales.
  - Obtained in excess of $10 million in new investment business through personal relationship development of major clients.
  - Reduced staffing levels by 20% saving $1 million in expenses, while increasing efficiency of operations, client satisfaction and sales volumes to achieve 50% net income growth.

- Successfully planned and led an amalgamation project of two major full-service branches with a combined staff of 150 and client base of 35,000 accounts. Orchestrated administration logistics, staffing considerations, ongoing sales effectiveness and client satisfaction.
- Introduced effective risk management strategies, reducing non-performing loan dollar volumes by 13%.

PROFESSIONAL EXPERIENCE - Financial Institution (1973-1993)

Branch Manager - Calgary, Alberta (1990-1994)

District Manager (Central Region) - Brandon, Manitoba (1988-1989)

Manager, Human Resources - Vancouver B.C. (1986-1987)

Senior Manager, Head Office Retail Loan Division (1984-1985)

Manager, Regional Retail Loan Operations (1982-1983)

Inspector, International Audit and Control Division (1980-1981)

Senior Account Manager, Corporate Lending (1976-1979)

Account Manager, Commercial Lending (1974-1975)

Various developmental and administrative positions (1973)

EDUCATION

Bachelor of Arts, University of Calgary (1972)
Executive Development Program, Banff School of Management (1991)
Fellow - Institute of Canadian Bankers (1981)
Various internal leadership, marketing and human resource studies

PERSONAL

Member - Chamber of Commerce (1989 - Present)
Commercial Campaign Coordinator - Calgary United Way (1992)

REFERENCES

References available upon request.

Example Number Three - Chronological

CRAIG BROADVIEW
139 Active Way
Halifax, Nova Scotia H6L 2C5

902-555-2002

Objective

"To assume a General Management position where my proven and wide ranging management abilities can lead a diverse group of employees in achieving and exceeding aggressive manufacturing targets for a regionally based corporation."

Key Qualifications

- Leadership through team building
- Excellent organizer and communicator
- Results orientation with strategic focus
- Conceptual thinker and proven problem solver

Professional Experience - International Conglomerate Inc.

General Manager - Production (1987-1994)

Staff Engineer (1985-1986)

- Developed and directly managed national capital expenditures budgets (facilities and equipment) in excess of $7.5 million annually, from design stages through to construction, installation and start-up.
- Introduced computer aided drafting (C.A.D) while coordinating facilities construction projects ranging from $100,000 to $5 million, consistently completing projects on time and within budget.
- Overviewed regulatory requirements to ensure compliance in: health, safety, environmental protection and transportation logistics. Injury frequency reduced by 68% over eight years
- Implemented national Production and Engineering meetings, fostering improved communications, cooperation and effectiveness.
- Initiated concept of team focused production units contributing to achievement of every manufacturing target in all three plant locations between 1992 and 1994.

Professional Experience - Industrial Engineering Services Ltd.

Industrial Engineering Consultant (1985)

- Acted as internal engineering consultant for five business groups within the company, investigating introduction of emerging technologies to enhance manufacturing procedures.
- Completed a four month manufacturing process study, recommending changes which yielded annual savings in excess of $300,000.

Professional Experience -Multinational Inc.

Industrial Engineer (1979-1984)

- Designed and coordinated ongoing feasibility studies aimed at identifying material utilization waste and production scheduling inefficiencies.
- Assessed data and redesigned material utilization & production flows, achieving consistently improved scrap ratings and optimum efficiency.
- Introduced a PC based production planning system, yielding cost and personnel complement reductions.
- Interfaced with and trained hourly employees to assume increased responsibilities for daily production targets, resulting in record output for 1983 and 1984.

Education and Professional Associations

Bachelor of Applied Science - University of Toronto (1979)
Public Speaking - Brown College - In progress
Registered Professional Engineer in Ontario and Nova Scotia
Member - Associations of Professional Engineers of Ontario (A.P.E.O.)
Director, Industrial Accident Prevention Association (I.A.P.A) Industry Class 13

Personal

Volunteer - Big Brothers of Halifax (1990 to Present)
Fluency in French

References

References available upon request.

Chapter 8

CAMPAIGN PREPARATION

In the earlier chapters of this book, it was suggested one of the toughest assignments you would ever face in your career would be the job of finding a job. To this point, all your efforts have been directed toward focusing on what you want to do. We are going to devote the balance of this book to waging an all out campaign, aimed at securing the right new position.

The following pages will be peppered with one word - NETWORKING. It is doubtful you will find anyone who can categorically tell you who first coined the phrase but you can be assured effective networking is the means of reaching the successful conclusion in your job search.

Before dashing off to network, it is important to have a firm grasp about what networking really means. Perhaps the best place to start is by illustrating what is NOT networking.

1.   Networking is not running hither, thither and yon, distributing your resume in hopes that someone will extend you a job offer.

2.   Networking is not preparing an exhaustive list of prospects
        and then asking them for a job.

Most people agree wholeheartedly with the concept of networking,
until asked to define networking. Usually the "people meeting"
factor is threaded into a fumbling attempt to define the illusive
word and occasionally some mention will be made of the fact you
should do it all the time.

The truth of the matter is there is no good dictionary definition for
networking in the context of the job search. For the purposes of the
upcoming chapters we will not attempt a definition but the
following statement will receive constant reference and attention:

"NETWORKING IS NOT JUST A PROCESS....

....NETWORKING IS A STATE OF MIND."

Again, before getting your campaign underway, let me impart
some background research which may assist you in understanding
why networking is so vital if you want to run a job search
campaign aimed at yielding proper and positive results.

In large measure, jobs come from four major areas: ad-
vertisements, facilitators, direct mailings and the hidden job
market. It is generally accepted that advertised openings allow you
to tap into about 5% of available positions. Facilitators and direct
mailings provide access to another 15% and positions in the so-
called "hidden job market" represent the residual. That's right -
80% - give or take a few percentage points. These statistics do
vary because of economic conditions and you will generally find
the figures attributed to the hidden job market will be nearer the
80% level during a recessionary period.

Let me make a point at this juncture. While you should penetrate
all those sectors, you should also be constantly aware of what

proportion of your time is being spent on each area. It does not take a mathematical whiz kid to tell you that if you are concentrating 75% of your "hours of business" on answering career ads and connecting with search firms or agencies that your well-meaning efforts are disproportionately focused.

Prior to mapping out an actual campaign, it is important to appreciate some background regarding each of these major categories.

Advertising

There are some realities about career ads which are important to understand. Indeed this information reinforces the need to tackle the hidden job market.

Corporations are more conscious of cost restraints today than ever before and advertising is extremely expensive. As a result, many companies delay advertising until they have exhausted every other recruitment avenue. Advertising is not always done simply to fill one vacancy.

So why do companies advertise and what impact can this have on you, the job seeker? In most instances, companies truly have a vacancy and they need to go to the market. Rest assured they will be flooded with resumes and the corporation will expend a considerable amount of time in making the right selection. These facts are important for you to bear in mind because you can be up against a massive amount of competition and the hiring process is not going to be particularly fast.

Some organizations still have a policy of advertising externally, thereby allowing themselves the opportunity to check internal candidates against the outside market. If the intent is to select the best person for the job, you have a genuine opportunity. On the other hand, if such a practice is driven primarily by a desire to keep internal candidates on their toes, all respondents have an uphill battle against the already known commodities from within.

Conversely, other organizations periodically like to fill up their "resume hopper" by placing fairly generic ads. In all fairness, they usually have an actual vacancy to fill and in these scenarios, even placing well up in the selection process can be a significant plus to you for potential future openings. However, in this scenario, you must decide upon the sincerity and validity of the age old phrase "... but we will keep your resume on file for other opportunities." This stock response can be found in many reject letters but for someone who has adopted networking as a state of mind, this can be a long-term opportunity to pursue and cultivate.

All that to say, responding to career ads is an important part of your job search. It can also be extremely aggravating because you have such limited control. In subsequent chapters, we will delve more thoroughly into the effective ways of approaching this portion of your overall strategy.

Facilitators

There are several factors to bear in mind when dealing with the third party facilitator, more commonly known as a search firm or agency. The first thing to remember is they do not work for you.

Search firms are typically on retainers and they are exclusively contracted by a corporate client to seek out and identify a short list of potential candidates to fill a specific vacancy. In most of these situations, there is a considerable amount of background work done with both the corporate client and the prospective candidates to ensure there will ultimately be a good fit between potential employer and employee. The good search firm has nothing to gain by putting forward candidates which are not a perfect fit.

Agencies work on a slightly different concept known as a contingency basis. In other words, they are paid by the corporate client if and when that organization selects a person put forward by the agency. In such scenarios, your "file" could well be in the hands of several potential employers at one time.

From your vantage point, it can be extremely advantageous to develop a good rapport with reputable search firms and agencies. Again, do not think for a moment either are working for you. Similarly, do not assume that by sending a letter and a resume to every search firm and agency in the yellow pages that you can then sit back and wait for your phone to ring off the hook.

These firms are inundated with literally thousands of resumes a year and even if they have a sophisticated cataloguing system, there is no guarantee your resume will be resurrected when an apparent good fit comes along. Your best approach is to treat these third party facilitators as just another good networking opportunity.

Direct Mailing

If you ask five people for their definition of direct mailing, you are more than likely to receive five different answers. The responses will vary from sending pro forma letters to a long list of company presidents to a much more tightly focused mailing, directed at selected people and companies.

Direct mailings can give you a short-lived sense of accomplishment, simply by virtue of the volume of paper you generate but if you are working on the assumption a mass mailing will precipitate incoming phone calls and job offers, you are in for a rude awakening. Companies are flooded with such information and in the vast majority of cases, they simply do not have the resources to even acknowledge receipt.

On the other hand, if you want to target specific companies or industries, a direct mailing campaign (as part of your overall job search strategy) may have some merit. To be most effective, the letters must be personalized and you must follow up. Lobbing resumes into the market place will simply not yield positive results. Letter #7 in the Appendix - Sample Letters will provide you with a sense of the most effective method of tackling direct mailings.

In essence, a well-planned and researched direct mailing is a less formal approach to networking, if you follow through with a personal contact. If you think you can avoid networking by sending out hundreds of letters, you are wrong. Clearly, a follow-up phone conversation is better than a letter alone and a direct mailing followed up with a face to face meeting is even better yet. In the latter case, you have really turned direct mailing into a networking opportunity.

Generally, direct mailings are not as effective as true networking but they are worth considering if you want to communicate with a larger number of people in a short period of time.

The Hidden Job Market

In order to effectively tackle the hidden job market, you must have a sound appreciation for what it is and how it works.

The driving force behind the hidden job market can be summarized in one word - CHANGE! Take a moment to reflect back on your previous employers while reading through the following scenarios. In each case, change has caused an opportunity to emerge from the hidden job market.

-        When the company's Chief Financial Officer took early retirement, the corporation abolished his position and redistributed many of his functions to other departments.

But, the company did hire a less senior accounting type. An opportunity was created but not necessarily for a person at the Chief Financial Officer level.

- A company was forced to significantly reduce operating expenses and to streamline their operation. They targeted a 15% work force reduction in the middle management ranks. When they took a final look at the revised organizational structure, they discovered only 80% of the management employees had the required skills, abilities and fit to fill the newly designed positions. As a result, they reduced the work force by 20% and then set about filling the additional vacancies. Again, opportunities were actually generated by a downsizing and change.

- A company had been losing market share for the past three years and was viewed as being in trouble. The new President was convinced the company approach was correct but the players were wrong. The preconceived notion on the street was they would not be hiring because they were encountering problems. In reality, they were on the verge of making significant staffing changes to bring on new people who were a better fit. The result - yet another possible set of opportunities.

- Another company was teetering on the brink of bankruptcy but at the last minute it was purchased by a competitor. What appeared to be a poor prospect for employment opportunities became an ideal situation because of change.

- Other organizations come to the conclusion that contracting out certain work is far less expensive than carrying a full-time employee. The newly created contract work may not be full-time but these situations can create interesting opportunities for the more entrepreneurial job seeker.

The examples of why positions become available are endless. New positions, altered responsibilities in existing positions, contract work for specific projects, change for the sake of change, change due to refocusing and the list goes on.

There are four things to remember in your job search:

1.   Make no assumptions - do your research.

2.   Changes are constantly occurring - even in poor economic conditions.

3.   Changes yield opportunities - if you are networking.

4.   Networking is not just a process - it is a state of mind.

With those words of wisdom etched in your mind, let us move on to how you can go about planning and implementing your job search campaign.

Networking

One of the primary reasons for a failed job search relates back to two words mentioned earlier - organization and research. Most people have the desire to find new employment but they lack the structure which can efficiently deal with the flood of new information needed to run an effective campaign.

The next few pages are devoted to explaining how this can be done and why it is critical. Part of the process involves recording and storing information and the sample formats provided are simple hard copy pro formas for your consideration. That is not to say you can not modify the basic layouts to suit your own preferences and needs, either on paper or through a computer program.

Before you start networking, you need to spend some time looking at who you know. If there was ever a time to invoke free thinking and a brainstorming mentality, it is now.

If you have begun your networking list, pull it out now. If you have not, grab a pen and paper and start jotting down people's names. And do not make the assumption that "good old so and so" should not be on the list because they likely can not help you. There will be plenty of time for refinements, additions and deletions later.

This is not a list of people who can hire you - it is a list of people who can possibly assist you in developing an effective network which will lead you either directly or indirectly to decision-makers. Just to aid your memory and get you started, or re-started, here is a list of a few groupings which might be of assistance:

- Family
- Friends
- Business associates from your last job
      - bosses, peers, and subordinates
- Business associates from previous jobs
- Ex classmates
- People from your church or lodges
- Professional associates
- Club members
- Previous customers and suppliers
- Conventions and conference participants
- Your doctor, dentist, lawyer and accountant

Remember, networking is not just a process, it is a state of mind. From this moment forward, you will need to reprogram yourself to look at life differently. Whether consciously or sub-consciously, you want to be constantly attuned and alert to expanding your network. Your conversations and your surrounding can act as catalysts in adding to your networking list.

-       A casual conversation with a friend may bring forth the name of a forgotten colleague.

-       An advertising billboard might strike a cord about someone who worked for a particular company and you met that person at a convention.

-       Someone might offer assistance simply by saying "Gee, you should get in touch with..."

Preparing this list is not a one-shot affair. Do a little family brainstorming to make certain you have not forgotten anyone and review the list frequently. You will find this constant referral will yield other possibilities.

When you have got the basic list started, transcribe it on to a central directory of one kind or another. The format of the NETWORKING DIRECTORY illustrated in the Appendix - Graphics & Forms # 3 is quite basic but let me give you some understanding about the rationale behind the layout.

-       Networking is primarily about people not companies. By leading off with the name of your contact on the Networking Directory, you will force yourself to remember the person. This should also apply to the Networking Directory Supplement we will discuss later.

-       The next most used bit of information will be that person's phone number. Following that data, you will want to record their title or area of responsibility, as well as the name of their company or organization - if applicable.

-       The "Referred By" column becomes valuable as you expand your network and want an easy means of recalling who put you in touch with your new contact.

-      The priority column will change as you get more into your
       job search but in the initial stages, you will be setting some
       priorities which will allow you to better manage volumes.
       You can not do everything at once. Hold off filling in your
       1, 2, 3 and T ("T" for test) ratings until you have read the
       section on selecting primary targets.

-      If you have an interest in a particular company but no
       specific contact, at least record the firm's name for future
       reference. The gaping blank in the first column is a great
       memory jogger to remind you to seek out a contact at a
       later date.

Establishing a Networking Directory allows you to map out and
constantly control your campaign at a glance.

Selection of Primaries

Unless you have an extraordinarily hot lead which requires
immediate attention, you should choose five or six contacts to test
your own approach to networking. There are some general rules of
thumb which you should consider when selecting these test cases
and they are as follows:

-      You should be personally at ease speaking to these people.

-      Similarly, you should be able to confide in them,
       explaining that you are developing your approach to
       networking.

-      They should be the type of individual who would freely
       offer constructive criticism.

As possible examples, you may wish to consider a close business
associate, a personal friend, a relative or even a previous boss who
may have been a mentor. Having selected a few "T's" for the

priority column, review each additional name in your Networking Directory. This is not a sophisticated process and common sense should prevail.

What you want to accomplish is the identification of no more than twenty "1's" or primary contacts. If you try to go beyond that figure, as a novice networker, you are apt to discover all too quickly you have more on your platter than you can comfortably manage at one time. It is very easy to add more names but if you begin with too many contacts, you can run the risk of handling them poorly, thereby wasting a great networking opportunity.

Categories "2" and "3" simply are a means of segregating the remainder, bearing in mind the 2's should generally be the contacts you will elevate to 1 status as you begin to work through the list.

Do not make the mistake of equating the 3's with people who are of no use to your job search. These just happen to be the contacts who could be valuable but they are a little lower on the first cut of your priority list.

Based on personal experience and conversations with countless numbers of people who have been job seekers, there are certain times when you really feel in control. The first occasion is when you can truly admit you have put your previous employer in the past, the second time is when you comfortably settle on an objective or job focus, and the third is when you put the finishing touches on a well-crafted resume. The fourth is when you have completed the initial working draft of your Networking Directory.

Take a minute and look at it. You should take a great deal of pride in the completion of this first organized phase of your networking strategy. But don't get too cocky! Remember, you have a few blanks to fill in and your new objective is to constantly be adding more potential contacts, whether they spring from you memory or through asking for referrals. Review the Networking Directory daily and keep the information current and organized.

Networking Directory Supplement

Now, if you were a military commander, you would have the luxury of a war room where you could plaster each wall with your Networking Directory and supplemental information. Even if you had the space and the inclination, that would not necessarily be the most effective method of staying organized and recording the more detailed research which is required in a job search campaign.

It is important to have a supplemental record to maintain critical data and subsequent notes. The Networking Directory Supplement, illustrated in the Appendix - Graphics & Forms # 4, is used for this purpose. You can keep this in hard copy or on the computer. Do not be limited by this particular design - it is a proven format but adjust it to suit your personal job search requirements.

Words of advice: take the time to fill out the Networking Directory Supplements properly and completely. If you call a company to confirm an address or the spelling of a name, make an effort to also confirm other information like direct phone numbers, fax numbers and exact titles. The Networking Directory Supplement also acts as your ongoing record of discussions, phone conversations and any other germane details.

If you think this is overkill, remember that during the course of your job search you could be networking with upwards of 150 people, many of whom you have not met before. The most common error for a beginner is to think you can and will recall all the details, only to find you are confusing one person or situation with another. Keep organized and your campaign will run smoothly.

Over and above your Networking Directory Supplement, you will always have other information such as copies of correspondence, news articles, annual reports and other such material. You have some choices in terms of handling this material but you likely want all the hard copy in one place so you can refer to it easily or perhaps even take it to meetings.

Inexpensive file folders are one simple system - one per contact - or you can hole punch everything and keep it in alphabetical order in a couple of large ring binders. Whatever method you decide upon, drive it off the individual contact's name. Company names may be easier to recall but you want to force yourself to remember the person.

The Newspaper

Many people limit their networking activities to the individuals they know or to the referrals they garner from their original contacts. In reality, there is another major source which provides an almost unlimited supply of information and possible networking leads - the newspapers.

If you are a sporadic newspaper reader, commit to become an avid reader. Better yet, if you are an avid fan of the newspaper, become a voracious reader. There is a natural inclination for job seekers to gravitate toward career ads in the newspaper but the entire paper needs to be perused with great care, each and every day.

Reading the paper on a daily basis ensures you keep current and that makes perfect sense when you consider all companies want to hire well-informed people. More importantly, you will find there is a flow or sense of continuity when you read thoroughly and regularly. Face it, you need to constantly be on top of what is happening in the business world, particularly when you are temporarily out of the day-to-day loop.

Perhaps the biggest challenge attached to reading the newspaper is to train yourself to read it differently. Most of us scan a paper for information which we anticipate will be supplied - stock quotes, sports scores, a recap of some major event, your horoscope or maybe a favorite columnist.

What you really want to do is start reading for opportunities. Not long ago, an article appeared in the local paper, announcing the appointment of a new President of a Canadian fast food chain. By the time you read the first paragraph you knew this company was rocketing toward major changes. Sizable reductions in staff were on the horizon and several locations would be closed.

On the surface you might conclude prematurely that this was not a company which you would ever consider including in your Networking Directory. Wrong assumption!

The head line proclaimed the incoming President's comments about staff reductions. But, if you took the time to dissect the article more carefully, several opportunities became evident and all of these were driven by change.

The new boss was committed to implementing an innovative marketing strategy, accompanied by a totally reworked advertising campaign. The outlets which were not being closed were to be physically redesigned and over a two year period these locations would be converted to a high tech computer system intended to streamline everything from inventory control to daily sales analysis. Topping off all these changes would be a renewed dedication to true customer service, delivered by a highly trained group of caring employees.

Would it be fair to conclude that this firm might be on the lookout for some new talent to drive their strategic concepts forward to tactical realities?

The skeptics reading this book might be apprehensive about the worth of closely scrutinizing the content of the newspaper, other than the traditional search through the career ads. Do yourself a favor and for one entire week, read the paper from start to finish. At the very least you will be better informed and in all probability you will begin to identify situations which could translate into opportunities for you.

Let the publishers, editors and writers assist you in the research phase of your job search and expand your network at every opportunity.

Chapter 9

NETWORKING

To this point, you have been getting prepared but the day arrives when you must turn all the planning into action and activity. As noted earlier, "Networking is not just a process - it is a state of mind" and the entire concept of networking is predicated on four basic premises:

1.   Gather useful information by meeting people.

2.   Constantly expand your network.

3.   Showcase your wares.

4.   Position yourself as a solution.

While networking is not just a process, there are some logical steps which must be followed if your job search is to be successful. Also, you can not lose sight of focus, organization, research and activity.

In this chapter we are going to concentrate on the following components of networking:

-       Preliminary staging for the networking meeting
-       Telephone follow up

Subsequent chapters will thoroughly address the issues and complexities of the following:

-       The meeting
-       Initial follow-up to the meeting
-       Resultant proposals for service

Preliminary Staging of Networking Meetings

In a later chapter you will find a comprehensive review of basic letter writing, as well as a complete set of sample letters. With a little creativity on your part these letters can easily be adapted to every situation - right from setting up a networking meeting to thank you letters which will position you to continue your networking into your next job and beyond.

The written form of communication will invariably set you apart from other job seekers. Some say letter writing is a dead or dying art form and unfortunately, those critics may well be correct. That said, well-crafted correspondence will open doors for you. Regrettably, this situation exists because quality letters are an exception today rather than the norm.

The other reason for stressing the importance of letter writing is simply because most people are adverse to making cold calls. Of all the people who are in the midst of a job search, only a handful of skilled communicators can run an effective career transition, solely by phone and one-on-one conversations.

Do not be mislead, telephone calls and face-to-face dialogue are a huge part of networking but effective written communications can and will ease the door open for meetings. Similarly, good correspondence will allow you to demonstrate and illustrate those skills which cause you to stand out from the crowd.

With this in mind, turn to the Appendix - Sample Letters # 1 and 2. These are stock type pieces of correspondence which you will want to dispatch prior to following up by phone to secure a networking meeting. Both are intended to be direct and to the point but more importantly, they set the stage for your subsequent call so the receiver has some indication of why you are attempting to get in touch.

The first example clearly gives you an edge because you are referencing a mutual contact. A person seeing this type of letter can do one of two things. They can check you out in advance by communicating with the referenced person or they can mentally accept the importance and credibility of your request by virtue of the fact that they respect the judgment of the mutual associate you have mentioned.

Looking at the letter in the Appendix - Sample Letters # 2, this situation is definitely more of a cold call than the first illustration. Like the first letter, this one paves the way for a follow up call. While it does not give you the advantage of a reference, it places you in a positive light with the recipient. These short but complete letters provide:

- An introduction
- A very brief history
- An explanation of what you want
  - information from an expert
- A statement concerning what you don't expect - a job
- A specific follow-up plan
- An acknowledgment of the person's busy schedule

Now for those of you who still think that grabbing the phone and making calls to unknown networking prospects is the best course of action because you avoid the waste of time caused by researching and writing letters - stop and reflect on the probable reaction of the recipient of such a letter!

Letter writing is by no means a guarantee that you will get through when you call or that you will ultimately secure a networking meeting. But, when your follow up call comes through, the chances of a positive response are significantly enhanced by your preliminary spade work.

And if you do not like making phone calls in the first place, you will feel much more comfortable in referring to your recent correspondence versus simply leaping into a dialogue with a stranger.

One last word of advice prior to moving to the telephone call. The people you want to reach are extremely busy and your letter has specifically stipulated when you intend to make contact. You cannot control the mail system but most of us have a sense about delivery times. It is preferable to have your letter arrive on a Thursday or Friday. The follow up date should be the following Monday. Timing is important and what usually will happen is the recipient will glance at the letter and automatically place it in the "Things to do on Monday" pile because of the date you have recorded.

On Monday, the letter could be given a second reading which will be more thorough. The highly organized person will likely toss it into next Friday's diary, working on the assumption if you do not call by then, you have failed to meet your own commitment.

Keep your job search organized. You do not want to blow a great opportunity because you were not disciplined enough yourself to make the phone call within the specified time frame.

The Phone Call

It is time to pick up the phone and make the first call!

Indeed, you have a stack of twelve letters in front of you that all say you are going to be in touch this week. Can you be the only person in the world who is so nervous about something as seemingly simple as making a dozen calls? The reality is that very few people truly relish making calls of this nature.

To make matters worse, today's telephone technology appears to place even more hurdles in front of you, further distancing you from the person you want to reach. It was bad enough when you had to do battle with an overprotective secretary or heaven forbid the central switch board but now you are increasingly faced with something called Voice Mail.

Even in the late 80's you did not encounter many companies with impersonal phone systems but as organizations pressed toward fewer and fewer support personnel, the number of voice mail systems increased dramatically. Some estimate that two thirds of today's business calls magically disappear into a machine - a machine which records, remembers and feeds back:

-       When you called
-       How you spoke
-       What you had to say
-       The inflection in your voice
-       The tone of your voice
-       Your questions
-       Your queries
-       And sometimes, your answers

The receiving party can save your words of wisdom and play them back as often as they want. Even worse, you can be deleted by the touch of a button.

Perhaps the foregoing paints a bleak picture but given how critical effective communication can be to your job search, it is important to understand what you are up against and how you can turn the electronic monsters to your advantage.

During a recent session on "Taming Today's Telephone Technology" participants were polled to inquire about their perceptions of the most common road blocks in getting through to the person they were calling. Here are the top six answers in random order:

- The person is never in
- They never seem to return calls
- The voice mail is always on
- The secretary always answers and screens calls
- There is no apparent alternative to the voice mail
- I simply don't like making the calls!!!

Actually, the last item on the list was by far the number one road block. When you couple that fact with not reaching one of your first three or four intended networking prospects, it is not such wonder you begin to resent the phone and become totally exasperated with the whole job search process. Wrong approach! You are letting the phone system run your campaign. Instead, look at the options you have when a voice mail kicks in:

1.   Hang up
2.   Listen and hang up
3.   Listen and punch zero for a real person
4.   Leave a message

Try option two and see what you can learn that may be of value before you choose options three or four. Here are a few examples of what you can glean from the telephone monster:

- In most cases, the voice mail will give you the pronunciation of the person's name and you are apt to get a sense about what first name they use. Is it a Bill or a William, a Pat or Patricia?

- Many people are so tied to their voice mail system that they record new messages at least once a day. This can be important for you if the message suggests when they are likely to return to the office.

- Just based on the flow of the recorded message, you can usually determine if the person is a regular user or even a strong advocate of a voice mail system. If they are, you are being given a signal that they are comfortable with conducting business via recorded messages. In some cases, you can actually set up a networking meeting without even talking to a real person.

- In other situations, the message will provide valuable information about the names and numbers of other people close to the person you are calling. Record this information in the event you want to try and reach the person's secretary or other associates.

- Quite often, frequent voice mail users will even go as far as to say where they are, if they are out of town and when they will be back. Or, whether or not they are going to be picking up messages.

By taking the time to listen, you will learn a great deal more about your potential contact. You might want to simply listen to his or her message, hang up, gather your thoughts and then call back to leave a well articulated, professional recording.

While a voice mail at the other end of the line may not grant you a meeting, you can easily and effectively showcase some of your wares by re-emphasizing the points in your initial letter, preparatory to an actual person to person discussion.

Before looking at a possible sample of what you might say in a recorded message, let's highlight what you want to get across:

- Who you are and when you phoned
- Why you called
- What information you want to impart
- What action you intend to take - if any
- What action you want taken by the recipient

The following monologue is a basic example and only an example. Take the time to craft your message so it truly sounds like you and test it on a home tape recorder or even by phoning your own answering machine. Keep the message length to 60 or 70 seconds. You do not want the receiver of your message to reach for the delete button if you sound like you are going to ramble on forever!

Extra time and effort will pay dividends as this trial run will not only ensure your recorded messages are crisp and to the point but you will slowly build up your confidence for those occasions when you immediately reach the person you are calling. The points you want to get across are almost identical, with the exception of the interaction of a two-way conversation and of course, your request for a meeting. And the message you leave on the voice mail should go something like this:

Hi Bill (Good Morning / Hello Mr. Smith)

This is Ray Price calling and it is Monday morning the 20th.

I am phoning to follow up on my letter of September 14th.

You may recall, Alan Jones had suggested I get in touch with you.

As I mentioned in my letter, I am in the midst of changing careers and I would appreciate the opportunity to get your professional observations on a few matters, relating to.............

Bill, let me stress, I am not looking for a position with your organization but I am very interested in gathering some much needed information.

I recognize your schedule is hectic but when your time permits, I'd appreciate you calling me back at 4 1 6 - 5 5 5 - 1 1 1 1.

(Optional) - If I am not in, please leave a message and I will return your call as soon as possible.

(Optional) - I should add, I will not be available on Thursday of this week.

Thank you for your time and I hope we will be able to connect in the very near future.

In the live situation, your side of the conversation will be very similar but the conclusions will be modified along these lines:

Thank you for taking the time to speak with me on the phone and I look forward to seeing you at 2:00 on Monday the 27th.

The phone is truly your life line when it comes to networking and it is for this reason that so much emphasis has been devoted to such a seemingly straight forward process. Over and above what we have already reviewed, let me leave you with a few other tricks of the trade which you may find useful.

The Secretary

Yes, there are still secretaries in the business world and they deserve the utmost respect. Go out of your way to develop a friendly and genuine rapport because if you are flip or tactless with them, you will substantially diminish your chances of ever getting through to your contact.

When you leave a "live" message to have your contact return a call, automatically offer some detail about why you are phoning. Often times a simple reference to your earlier correspondence will be sufficient. After two or three pleasant exchanges with the secretary you can even garner some information about the best time to catch your illusive contact.

The Internal Phone Trick

Many phone systems differentiate between outside incoming calls and internal incoming calls. If your contact appears to be evading you, try phoning a number which is one or two digits removed from that of your contact. A simple "Oh, I'm sorry, I must have dialed the wrong number, would you mind transferring me to ..." could get you through.

Keeping Track

In the "notes" section of your Networking Directory Supplement, keep careful track of when you called and whether or not you left a message with a person or with a voice mail. A simple 6m or 6vm will indicate you phoned on the 6th and it will also note what type of message you left.

This record keeping is important to gauge when you should follow-up if your request for a return call goes unanswered. If you have left a message which is out of the ordinary, jot down the essence of what you said, such as: "Bill, I wanted to let you know I returned your call from earlier today but I am going to be out of town until and 8th and I will give you a call when I return."

Good Times to Call

Sorry, no pat answers to this question. That said, you can experiment by trying calls early in the morning, over lunch or after normal business hours. Voice mail fanatics often turn the systems off in the early morning hours to accept internal calls from other early-rising work associates. Some may answer their own calls while support staff are away for lunch and many take the systems off service after 5:00 to facilitate incoming personal calls.

"I'm in the Middle of a Meeting...."

If you finally reach your contact but receive the above response, it is not the time to attempt an abridged version of your dialogue. Simply ask when it would be a good time to phone back. Maintain control of the calling process and then follow through exactly on time. Even if you fail to connect the second time, you have clearly demonstrated you were well organized and met your commitment. That can be just enough to cause a contact to return your next call promptly.

Recorded Message :
"I'm out of town for the next week."

Don't hang up. Use this as an opportunity to again demonstrate your professionalism by confirming you called as per your previous written commitment and indicate you will phone back, a couple of days after your contact returns to the office. You are suggesting you know how hectic it can be after being out of the office for an extended period of time and this acknowledges you have experienced similar circumstances in your past day-to-day work routine.

Telephone Guidelines at Home

In many cases, you will be receiving return calls at home and the family needs to understand the importance of not only the incoming phone calls but also what you are attempting to accomplish while on the phone. Set up some rules and regulations. Review them periodically, particularly with the children - whether they be pre-schoolers or teens. Just a few examples:

- During "business hours" keep family member calls to an absolute minimum.

- Keep the call duration short.

- Answer calls promptly and courteously.

- Don't summon Mom or Dad by the usual bellowing shriek:

     "It's for you!!!!!"

- Ensure messages are written down, not forgotten and promptly relayed.

Invest in some form of call answering at home, preferably with the option of picking up messages by remote. Most local telephone companies now offer this service at very reasonable rates. At least while you are involved in your job search, keep your greeting message business-like.

Making the Calls

Decide when you are going to make your calls, get organized with all your background material and GET STARTED! By making several calls in a row, you will find yourself developing a steady cadence and your confidence will build steadily with each message left and/or conversation.

Set yourself a realistic goal for the number of calls to be made. By getting them out of the way in a relatively short period of time, you leave the line free for incoming return calls. When you are finished, you can turn your attention to other details of your job search like letter writing or research.

During the time you are on the phone, try to work in a noise free environment where you have all of your information readily available. When you connect, visualize the person on the other end of the line, be yourself and carry on the discussions as though you were face-to-face.

In the event you receive an incoming call when it is not convenient for you, politely thank the person for returning your call but explain you are not able to speak at that moment and you will phone back in five minutes. There is little sense in burning the hamburgers on the barbecue and simultaneously blowing a perfectly good networking opportunity. Properly handled, the contact will appreciate the courtesy of a return call when you are able to devote your full attention to the matters at hand.

Be Up!

Any highly successful sales person will tell you that you must be UP to make good sales calls and that is exactly what you are doing - selling yourself. It is a fine line between not being up and procrastinating. Using the excuse "I'm not in the phoning mood" can not last for more than one or two days. If you go beyond, you are procrastinating and you should give yourself a shot of self-confidence by reviewing this chapter.

You might even ease yourself into a good telephone day by starting with a call to an old colleague or friend, just to get the blood flowing. Above all, *never* let a bad telephone day cause you to avoid meeting those commitments you made in an earlier letter or during a previous call.

Notes

Take rough notes while you are speaking with a contact and immediately transcribe the usual hen scratch to your Networking Directory Supplement. Even reject calls deserve write ups because you may need the information in the future.

If you do not accomplish the desired results during your call, ensure you conclude your conversation on a positive and polite note. You might well orchestrate another opportunity to see this person and at the very least, you always want to demonstrate your own professionalism and careful attention to detail.

In such cases, a further positive image can be solidified by using a written follow-up such as the one outlined in the Appendix - Sample Letters # 9. As noted earlier, stay organized and generate your correspondence in a timely fashion.

Some "Do Not's"

Avoid making calls from your car phone unless it is absolutely necessary. If you do, at least pull off the road, do not use hands free and be prepared with your notes.

Similarly, do not call a contact at their home or in their car, unless they have made the offer. Even then, it is not the best option because they may not be concentrating on what you have to say.

Persistence

Working the telephone part of your job search campaign can be one of the most exasperating experiences of your lifetime and it can also be one of the most rewarding. As any accomplished salesperson will tell you, never stop calling when you are on a roll. That old adage may be mostly myth but you can actually feel a heightened level of confidence after a good phone conversation and you will transmit that enthusiasm during your next call.

Networking phone calls are a challenge but they are almost always the precursor to an actual networking meetings where you can truly showcase your wares and gather more information. And perhaps this is a good time to offer some sound advice from Calvin Coolidge regarding persistence. Take a look at the quote on the next page - it is worth copying and posting beside your phone.

"Persistence"

"Nothing in the world can take the place of persistence. Talent will not; nothing is more common than unsuccessful men with talent. Genius will not; unrewarded genius is almost a proverb. Education will not; the world is full of educated derelicts. Persistence and determination alone are omnipotent."

                                        - Calvin Coolidge

Chapter 10

THE NETWORKING MEETING

"Well isn't this great - all the phoning has paid off and I have my first networking meeting scheduled. But what do I do now?"

As is so often the case in your job search, you no sooner clear one hurdle when another appears. For many, the new challenges are even more onerous because the entire experience is foreign. Few of us grab our "Indiana Jones" hat and recklessly rush into the unknown to start a new venture.

Networking or information gathering meetings can easily fall into this category, particularly if you still harbour an almost unbridled urge to rush into the meeting and ask for a job. Don't! If you do, you have compromised what you have said in your introductory letter and your initial phone conversation which orchestrated the meeting. Worse still, the answer to your question will be negative. If by some strange quirk of events there is a vacant position, ideally suited to you, your networking contact will let you know but within their own time frames.

One of the most often asked questions relative to not asking for a job is whether or not this is really an honest approach. The truth of the matter is you are researching new career opportunities - you have never said anything to the contrary. With that fact in mind, let's quickly look at a few things to remember.

- This meeting is not an interview
- You are gathering information and researching
- You are asking for input from an expert
- You are asking for guidance and direction
- You are searching for other information sources
- You might be validating your objective
- You are listening and storing data
- You want to expand your network
- You are looking for other contacts in the company
- You are NOT asking for a job!!!!
- But, you are showcasing your wares

Networking and the information gathering meeting are part of a continuum, they are not one-shot efforts. And that is why networking must become a state of mind and not simply a process.

Like all other components of your job search, the networking meeting is vital to landing a new position. As such, meticulous care is required before, during and after the meeting. Neglect any of these three steps and you run the risk of jeopardizing a good opportunity. If you follow the type of detail about to be described for the first half dozen meetings, it will soon become second nature. Doing it properly to begin with will establish a comfort level and you will form good habits.

Before the Meeting

Once you have secured the meeting, review all the material you have at your disposal. If you feel you do not have sufficient background information concerning the company, do a little more research. A trip to the local library will give you access to recent news items about the company and other available resource material from the library may offer further insight about the company's history.

Just as an aside, there is nothing more embarrassing than getting into a networking meeting and having your contact ask your opinion about a recently publicized news item concerning the company, only to find you have not been keeping pace with current business events. As stated earlier, if you are in the job search mode, part of your daily ritual must be a careful perusal of newspapers. You will find this becomes easier once you have established your Networking Directory which helps you to zero-in on pertinent reading.

If your meeting was aided along by having a referral from someone, give that person a call. They are part of your network and by keeping them apprised of your progress, you are re-enforcing the fact you are still actively involved in your search. At the same time, you can ascertain if your original contact has any further inside information which may be useful during your upcoming meeting.

Having refined your background information, jot down what you want to find out during the meeting. Indeed, these requirements will allow you to structure some specific questions which you will want to raise during the dialogue.

Let's stop here for a moment and address the whole issue of developing questions for your networking meeting. The first rule of thumb is to start with broad general questions and then begin to focus on more specific queries. Unfortunately for you, the conversation can take many twists and turns, simply because you can not control the responses which are given by your contact. But by preparing questions which will elicit the information you need, you are in a much better position to influence the direction of the discussions.

A little later in this chapter you will have an opportunity to review an example which will assist you in developing questions. Remember, you have three major goals during this meeting. First, you want to gather information. Second, you want to make a favourable impression and last but not least, you want to expand your network.

Speaking of making a favourable impression, double check one other detail before the day of the meeting. Companies have a bad habit of having more than one location. They may use one street address for their incoming mail but your contact could be situated in another building. Check!

Just prior to heading off to the meeting, you have two last minute items to handle. One is an image check and while most people become annoyed when this subject is broached, it is extremely important. The subsequent chapter on interviewing will address the subject in more detail. Another item on the agenda is straight forward. Leave yourself lots of time to ensure you are early. Improper preparation or arriving one minute before the appointment are two of the easiest ways to jeopardize a good meeting.

Now you might think it would be natural to leap right from here into the actual meeting. Not so fast - you still have to contend with the reception or waiting area. You can on occasion learn a great deal during your brief stay in the outer office.

In the vast majority of cases, your first contact with the company will be the receptionist. Properly handling yourself in this situation can afford you an opportunity to mentally prepare and set the tone for your visit. Introduce yourself, politely explain who you are, who you are to see and the time of your appointment. An upbeat and confident dialogue with the receptionist will set the stage for your introductory comments to your contact. Do not forget, your contact may at a later time casually question the receptionist about his or her impressions and observations.

By being early you allow yourself a few minutes to complete one last check of your notes and questions. Then, take time to absorb your surroundings and gather some peripheral information. If you are alert and attentive, it is amazing what you can glean from a ten minute wait in the reception area. Here are just a few examples.

-       What does the area tell you about the company's image? It can range from stark and functional to understated elegance or even palatial.

-       What about the employees who are moving through the area? Are they formal, informal, chatting, relaxed, intense, up beat, or sombre? Do they generally seem to dress in formal business attire, are they somewhat less formal or are they downright casual?

-       What, if anything, is displayed in the reception area? Are there products on display or are the walls covered with expensive looking art?

-       What are employees talking about and what can you gather from those snippets of conversations?

Any and all of your observations can significantly assist you in formulating a "feel" for the company.

The Meeting

Eventually, someone is going to appear and in most cases, your contact is likely to come and greet you in the reception area. If you have never met the person before, let them take the lead in introductions. This exchange is not only important in terms of initially building rapport but you can also clarify some potentially nagging questions. Let's look at a typical dialogue where Bill Smith is the contact and Ray Price is the guest.

Bill: *"Ray, I'm Bill Smith."*

Note, he is Bill and not William and he is inviting you to use his first name.

Ray: *"Good morning Bill, it is a pleasure to finally meet you in person."*

OR

Bill: *"Raymond, I'm Bill Smith."*

Ray: *"Good morning Bill, please call me Ray. It is a pleasure to meet you."*

Get the names straight now. This is going to become an ongoing relationship and you want to avoid any initial confusion.

If Bill is late, have a response ready that will set him at ease and also cause you to create the most favourable impression. Simple responses like those recorded below easily do the trick.

Bill: *"Ray, I'm Bill Smith, sorry for keeping you so long. My meeting ran into overtime."*

Ray: *"Good morning Bill, it is a pleasure to finally meet you in person."*

"No problem, I was just catching up on my reading."   or

"No problem, I was just admiring your offices."

The long walk down the hallway is not the place to start your formal conversation. That said, silence is not golden and you want to keep the chatter light.

Once you get to the actual office, you should be making an effort to assimilate the entire surroundings. Unless you are meeting off-site or in a boardroom, the contact's office can supply you with a wealth of information about the person. Do not forget, your network is in large measure based on people and you want to use every opportunity to quickly understand the personal side of your new contact.

For those of you who are un-observant let me give you a few tips on what you can learn when you walk into a stranger's office. Finding a new job is serious business but you can have a little fun with this type of amateur detective work and this seemingly mundane information can become extremely useful.

Marital Status?
        - Wedding ring, picture of spouse on credenza

Children?
        - Pictures or "refrigerator" art work

Divorced or Separated?
        - No ring and just photos of the kids

Athlete or Sports Enthusiast?
        - Sporting memorabilia

Education?
        - "Sheepskins" or certificates

Professional Affiliations?
        - Plaques and certificates

Hobbies / General Interests?
- Books, art work, pictures or other artifacts

Work Habits?
- Cluttered desk or the "clear vista"

Company Tenure?
- Plaques or pins

Stature within Company?
- Size of office, furniture, floor location

Computer Buff?
- Lived in look around computer station

Formal or Informal?
- Dress, posture, office lay out

These and a variety of other clues will allow you to instantaneously develop a sense about this person. You should file that information away for your immediate encounter and for future reference. Responding appropriately to these clues can significantly enhance the rapport building process.

Usually there are two items to deal with before the formal part of the meeting begins. Exchanging business cards is a good idea and on many occasions you will be offered a coffee. If you are a klutz by nature, politely decline the coffee by saying you have just had one but allow your contact the option of refilling his or her own cup. On the other hand, if you want some and feel at ease sipping a coffee and talking, take your host up of the offer. You are two business people getting together for a discussion, this is not an inquisition or an interview.

The issue of business cards deserves further comment. If you are reading this book, having a business card is as natural to you as carrying a pen. There is no mythical rule that says unemployed middle managers can not carry business cards. In fact, they are a well worthwhile investment and by making a few phone calls, you will be able to find an inexpensive supplier.

Spend the $30 or $40 and simply record your name, address and phone number. By the way, use your "known as" name - nothing is more aggravating than receiving a "William Smith" business card, only to find out that the presenter goes by Bill. Listing all your degrees can be pretentious but in some professional circles it is very important - use your own good discretion on this issue.

The Meeting Dialogue

Again, this is a meeting and not an interview. You are in control and for the most part, it is your agenda. There is no better way to prepare you for a networking meeting than to offer you a typical dialogue, with some editorial comment. The following will supply you with a structured format for your interaction with your various contacts.

The Meeting Dialogue - Rapport

"Bill, first let me thank you for taking the time to see me. I know Alan Jones said your schedule was very hectic these days."

- Small talk will occur throughout this segment
- Restate the name of your referral

"I think I had indicated when I phoned that I would only need about 30 minutes of your time but I can certainly understand if you have had to alter you schedule since we spoke."

- Wait for the signal
- If none, assume 30 minutes is OK

"Let me reemphasize one point, if I didn't make it clear when we last spoke, I am in need of some information but I am not here looking for a position with your company."

The Meeting Dialogue - Purpose

"I am looking for some input from you regarding your company and the xxxx industry in general. Alan felt you would be a good person to speak with, given your heavy involvement in this sector. I do have some specific questions to ask but perhaps if I quickly give you a bit of background information about me and an overview of my career objectives, the reasons for my questions will be more clear."

- Keep the background detail very short
- Simply state the objective you have developed

"Over the course of the past 15 years, I have worked for two companies in the xxxx industry and since 1988, my career has focused on ...."

"In the last month I have spent a considerable amount of time defining what I want to do and basically my objective is to...."

- Wait to see if any clarification is required
- Ask if it is OK to take notes
- Start with broad, general questions
- Move toward more specific questions

The Meeting Dialogue - Questions

"Bill, do you mind if I take a few notes?"

"To allow me to better understand the xxxx industry, can you give me your opinions in terms of some of the major changes and

challenges you envision taking place in Canada, during the course of the next three years."

"With those issues in mind, what action plans will your organization likely take to respond to those changes?"

"From your vantage point, are your competitors likely to respond in a similar fashion or are there other avenues which might be considered?"

"Let me just get back to the issue of competitors. If you don't mind my asking, who do you see as your major competition?"

"As I mentioned at the outset, my objective is to assume a position in.... Can you give me some insight on what trends or changes you see taking place in that sector."

"From the people perspective, what changes in skills and other requirements might you anticipate three years in the future?"

"And how will your company be handling the xxxx function in the future?"

"Given what we have discussed, I would certainly welcome your thoughts about my career objective and your advice regarding any changes that you might think are necessary."

Throughout the conversation offer your opinions when appropriate, when you truly agree and where you are on firm ground.

This is your opportunity to **showcase your wares**, not to show off!

The Meeting Dialogue - Recap / Close

"Bill, you have given me a great deal of valuable information. Correct me if I am wrong but based on what you have said, it would appear that:

> *1.*
> *2.*
> *3.*

"I will certainly review your information with the other data I have gathered. I don't have any other questions at the moment but would you mind if I gave you a call later, should I need any further clarification?"

"There is one other item that would be helpful. Based on our discussions today, can you suggest anyone else, either in your organization or elsewhere, that you feel could further assist me in gathering additional information?"

- If the answer is yes, get the details.
- If the answer is no....

"Well, if someone does come to mind, I would appreciate hearing from you."

Optional - *"Actually, if it would not be too much trouble, I would like to send you a copy of my resume and perhaps I could give you a call next week to quickly get your feedback".*

"Bill, I have taken up enough of your time and again, I have really appreciated your input. I will definitely follow up with Mr./Ms. ____. By the way, would you mind if I mentioned your name when I make contact? I will keep you apprised on my progress. If it is not

inconvenient, I will send you a copy of my resume, <u>simply for your records</u>."

- Don't linger

After the Meeting

You have done your prep work and you have had a good meeting. Do not stop there, the post meeting work is every bit as important as the first two stages. Your dedication to proper follow-up after the meeting is just another step to set yourself apart from all your competitors. And the technical procedures are really very simple:

- Transcribe your notes
- Prepare follow-up letter
- Diarize action items
- Communicate with your original contact
- Write new referrals
- Keep in touch with all your contacts

Whatever you do, do not rely on the rough notes you might have taken during your discussions. Those are highlights only and you will want to capture the details. The sooner you sit down to review the content of the meeting, the better. Grab a coffee and take the time to mentally retrace the entire networking meeting - right from your preparation through to the final hand shake. Record all your observations in your Networking Directory Supplement and critically evaluate what you did right and what you could improve upon.

If time permits, you should draft your thank you letter immediately, while the nuances of the conversation are still crystal clear in your mind. The suggested follow-up letter will give you a good example but let's review the basics. You want to extend a sincere thank you for: the meeting, your contact's time and their valuable information. To demonstrate your alertness to their commentary, you may want to highlight one or two specifics which were most helpful or germane to your inquiries. Confirming that you are going to follow-up on any suggested referrals illustrates your genuine interest in advancing your networking efforts.

Unless part of your networking agenda was to seek input about your resume (and there is nothing wrong with that approach in moderation) do not hand out your resume at the end of every meeting. Your resume is not some pizzeria advertising flyer to be thrust into the hands of every passerby by at the local mall. You have expended a considerable amount of effort in developing your resume and it deserves to be presented as a professional supplement to a personalized follow-up letter.

Finally, make certain you leave the door open with your contact by confirming a possible subsequent follow-up regarding unanswered questions or simply by keeping them apprised about your progress. By virtue of taking the time to meet with you, contacts now have a vested interest in you and on the other hand, you want to keep your name in front of them.

If you have even made a passing comment which can be construed as a commitment on your part, make note of it and diarize these action items. Then, follow-through. Take advantage of each and every possible opportunity to demonstrate your true sincerity and professionalism.

If you were originally referred to this contact by another, follow-through again. Depending on the circumstances, the follow-up could be as formal as a letter or as informal as a voice mail message saying the meeting went well and you received a great deal of valuable information.

Communicating with new referrals is simply a matter of adding to your Networking Directory and activating the networking steps all over again. Finally, map out and diarize how you intend to keep in touch with your contact.

Remember, networking is not a one-shot effort and you need a plan to maintain the contact. This can be done by confirming a meeting with the referral they gave you, by sending a final version of your resume, by forwarding copies of articles or by following through on some other issues you may have discussed.

Even for the most skeptical or reticent person, networking can be fun if approached in the proper manner. You will have great meetings, good meetings and downright poor meetings. But through planning, preparation and rehearsed execution, you will be astonished at how your networking skills will develop and improve in a short period of time.

Indeed, you will know when you have achieved a degree of proficiency in networking when you come to the realization that this approach not only applies to your job search but also to the ongoing expansion of yourself. You will soon come to appreciate how networking will allow you to capitalize on more business opportunities when you return to the work force.

"The greatest mistake you can make in life is

to be continually fearing you will make one."

- Elbert Hubbard

Chapter 11

THE PROPOSAL FOR SERVICE

There is no formula which equates a certain number of networking meetings with successfully landing a new job. The influencing factors are many and varied. Your profession, your personal commitment, local economic conditions, the type of industries in your locale, your degree of proficiency in networking and several other issues will dictate when you will achieve your goal.

But from time to time, you will sense or see the signs that simple networking needs to be progressed to the next plateau. Generally, this occurs after more than one session with a contact and you become aware their needs align with your interests and abilities.

If and when these situations arise, you are confronted with the need to take control and actively press forward, thereby potentially developing your own opportunity. These are not necessarily situations where a specific job is sitting vacant waiting for someone to hire you and deposit you into a ready-made position. In other cases, there may never be a permanent full-time job with the company but you could very well orchestrate a contract arrangement where you are the supplier of services.

Regrettably, you are not likely to find a pro forma for a proposal for service presentation, where you simply fill in the blanks. Content, layout, degree of analysis, length, sophistication of research and a multitude of other features will depend upon the company you wish to approach and to some degree, upon your own style. However, there are some basic elements which need to be incorporated into every proposal for service and we will address each of the following in greater detail:

- Accompanying Letter
- Situational Summary
- Desired Results
- Other Factors to Consider
- Suggested Course of Action - Benefit Analysis
- Compensation (optional)

For those of you who have hailed from national or international conglomerates, putting together a personal proposal for service can be somewhat unnerving. The concept may not be foreign to you but in your previous work life, you might have always enjoyed the comfort of using your ex-employer's standard or prescribed format. Staring at a blank piece of paper or monitor can be a perplexing experience. All of a sudden, you realize the true meaning of the word entrepreneur. Your product is you and your ideas.

Like good letter writing, formulating a proposal for service is not something which can usually be dashed off in an hour. It will need to be drafted, edited, expanded, researched and re-researched before you generate a polished presentation which fully satisfies your own requirements. Given the situation you intend to address, there may be a need for more than the basic components mentioned earlier but as a starting point, let's look at each of the usual major items.

The Letter

This piece of correspondence (See Appendix - Sample Letters # 15) has three primary functions. You want to capture the recipient's attention, recap what has already transpired and explain what future action you envision.

It is extremely important to appreciate the fact your contacts are not likely to specifically ask you for a proposal for service. The onus is usually on you to initiate action. Part of their methodology may be to wait and see if you have heard and understood their future requirements and whether or not you are assertive enough to act upon their subtle purchasing clues.

There is a risk involved in submitting a proposal for service because if you are simply relaying great ideas, the company can keep what you have transmitted and implement the actions on their own. With this in mind, you must weave you and your ideas together to ensure the viability of your suggestions are directly linked to you. In a similar vein, your letter might only include a comprehensive outline of the proposal for service and the expanded version can be tabled at a later and more appropriate time.

Situational Summary

During various meetings with your contact, you have been gathering and recording a great deal of information about the company. That data will be supplemented by the other research which you have been conducting.

This is a summary and as such it should be a concise recounting of pertinent historical factors, a synopsis of the direction the company is considering and a restating of that new goal. The following hypothetical example about a mortgage company will give you some further insight about the content and set up.

> *"The XYZ Mortgage Company was first incorporated in 1972 and it currently services both residential and commercial client requirements through a network of 50 locations in Canada, situated in all major cities and several smaller communities.*
>
> *While the XYZ Mortgage Company has been negatively impacted by the recent recession, the last audit of the portfolio suggests it is of better than average quality and all deteriorating situations are well in hand. The current dollar mix of mortgages is 60% commercial and 40% residential.*
>
> *Over the course of the next two years, the company wishes to realign the portfolio mix to a 50 / 50 ratio for commercial and residential business, while streamlining the entire administrative function to reduce operating costs by 15% from those levels recorded last year."*

The reader of a situational summary should be left with the sense that you have captured the essence of what is going on and what goals are envisioned for the future. It is not necessary to concern yourself with minute details because it is unlikely you will be privy to such sensitive information.

The Desired Results

In this section you wish to record what the company wants to accomplish. During your networking meetings, you will have likely garnered a reasonably good idea about their future focus, how they want to achieve these goals and generally what those goals are. Again, this is not a test because you are not an insider.

Not only do you want to capture their stated or implied desired results but you might want to plant a few ideas of your own to accentuate the fact you possess valuable insight which could be of benefit to the company. In most cases, it is wise to record the desired results in point form and taking the previous example a step further, the content may look something like this:

- *To achieve a 50 / 50 ratio in the portfolio by maintaining current commercial portfolio levels while significantly expanding the total residential outstandings.*

- *To streamline administrative activities by centralizing the process in selected centers where optimum cost savings can be achieved.*

- *To maintain current personnel complement numbers over the course of the next two years but to increase staffing in areas directly interfacing with the clients.*

- *To undertake a complete review of all demographic trends in an effort to identify the 30 most likely "fast growth" areas between now and the year 2000. **

- *To continue to provide high quality service to all existing customers.*

- *To reassess the viability and need for the existing network of office locations.*

* (Optional) Perhaps this item has never been raised in previous discussions but it seems sensible and it is something you might do. If the idea is already part of their plan, you come across as a well-informed industry specialist. If it was not, you have illustrated your ability to put forward innovative concepts for discussion.

Other Factor to Consider

This section affords you an opportunity to editorialize, bringing into play the industry research which you have gathered, either during your networking or as a result of specifically preparing for the proposal for service.

Your comments might well be linked to some or all of the desired results and you want to illustrate your additional understanding of factors which may need to be considered. The continuation of the previous example will illustrate how this can be accomplished.

> *"Based on XYZ's last annual report, the outstanding portfolio totalled $ million, with 60% being classified as commercial. If the commercial outstandings are to remain constant and if you wish to achieve a 50/50 ratio between commercial and residential outstandings, this will necessitate an increase in residential volumes of some $ million over the next two years. Given industry projections and current economic forecasts, this will require a larger commitment to the marketing of residential products, likely driven by an expanded and more sophisticated sales force.*

> *To coincidentally meet the objectives of zero growth in the total work force, administrative economies of scale will need to be implemented at an extremely early date to allow for personnel complement growth in those areas which will directly contribute to the expansion of the residential mortgage portfolio.*

> *Based on assumptions recently quoted in the June issue of "The Mortgage Industry Journal", it would appear the recession might well alter population growth patterns in several communities, thereby calling for the re-evaluation of long-term business viability in certain areas.*

While service to existing individual clients and communities is critical to sustain market share, the physical presence of a community office may not necessarily be the only means of servicing customers, particularly if the ten year projections for community growth are at levels which might not support the maintenance of a full-fledged office.

Recent technological advances suggest consolidated "back office" operations are becoming much more viable and earlier legitimate concerns about potential poor service to local clients have been minimized via various direct link-ups with larger, more efficient administrative service centers."

Suggested Course of Action / Benefits

In this segment, the presenter wants to convey some high level solutions which will further capture the interest of the reader, while also directly linking the writer to the solutions.

In other words: "Buy My Ideas - Buy Me!"

"Over the course of the past five years, I have been heavily involve in various restructuring processes, all aimed at maximizing administrative efficiencies in situations where a company has multiple office locations.

In my opinion, such re-engineering projects can not take place in isolation from the rest of the company. Decisions must be predicated upon overall long-term strategies, incorporating a number of issues such as the organization's desired image in the market place.

Based on our preliminary discussions, I do believe your aggressive objectives can be realized by implementing a coordinated plan, including the following components:

- A demographic study of growth areas
- Analysis of centralization benefits
- Identification of centralized sites
- Action plans focused on maximum efficiencies

As I indicated in my covering letter, I am impressed with the direction being taken by XYZ Company and I firmly believe securing my services would yield both short and long-term benefits for all concerned."

Putting forth a proposal for service is by no means a guarantee for a job or a contract but if you have read the situation and their needs correctly, you have positioned yourself as part of the solution. Indeed, you may have saved the company time and money by virtue of the fact they need not search any further for a remedy to their problem.

Just to be clear, proposals for service are not common place when your search is concentrated on securing a more traditional full-time position. But, there are circumstances which call for this type of pro-active approach and these situations become even more evident if desired career directions include project type work.

At the very least, a well thought out proposal for service which does not land you a job will have given you the chance to showcase your wares and positively influence your contact for future opportunities, either within their company or outside.

Chapter 12

RESPONDING TO CAREER ADS

Chapter Eight touched on the fact you want to remain alert to advertised openings, even though they represent a relatively small portion of available opportunities within the total job market.

In reviewing the entire issue of responding to career ads, people generally do a poor job in terms of pre-qualifying themselves, writing covering letters and following through. There seems to be a pervasive attitude which says: "See It! Send It! Sit & Wait!" Your chances of adding to your collection of reject letter will be greatly enhanced if you take this approach.

Like everything else, to be effective in responding to ads and getting to the interview stage, you must understand the background. Recognizing what goes on behind the scenes will significantly help you to cope with the often times exasperating experience of replying to a career ad.

Why do companies advertise? The initial assumption is they have a vacancy which they can not fill internally and that is often true, but not always. Some organizations have a policy that stipulates they will advertise externally before making a decision about internal candidates. It is difficult to disagree with this philosophy but it can be most perplexing for the job seeker who is fully qualified and is then rejected because the internal candidate has equal or even lesser credentials. That is not to suggest you should not be mindful of advertised opportunities but it is very important to understand the realities of the market.

Similarly, some companies like to fill up their resume hopper from time to time. They may select one person for a current vacancy and in these cases, they may genuinely mean it when they say "We have filled the position but you have just the right qualifications we are looking for and we will keep your resume on file for future openings." It is easy to become jaded about that response. On the other hand, if it is true and not just a polite way of saying no, you will wish to follow through with this company to maintain or enhance your exposure.

The issue of dealing with a career ad goes well beyond the written response. To give you a better overview of the entire process, the following pages will offer some additional background information, as well as specific suggestions aimed at helping you in responding to and following up on those ads which are worthy of your consideration.

Response Volumes

Particularly in a recessionary period, any company which advertises can expect to be inundated with tremendous volumes in response to an ad. Many companies advertise nationally, so you are not only competing with locals but also with a host of other prospective candidates. Again, that reality should not dissuade you from replying but rather, it does stress how important it is for you to set yourself apart from all the others. Your first concern is to get into the "Keeper" pile and that issue will be addressed later.

Another point to remember is speed is not a factor, although timeliness of your response is a consideration - particularly if the ad specifies a closing date. There is nothing to be gained by being the first envelope to land on the reviewer's desk. Indeed, if getting your letter out on the same day as the ad appears is your primary motivation, you are apt to have rushed the preparation of the accompanying letter.

The Ad Itself

Many people fail to appreciate that career ads are not simply words on a page, intended to connect the employer with prospective employees. To some degree they are advertising and while they may appear to have a captive market, the reality is that companies are attempting to sell their organization and the position which is available. Why would they be advertising if they were not looking for purchasers?

Take the time right now to grab a career section and quickly read a half dozen ads. Many of the inserts have been professionally prepared at no small expense to the company. And don't all those companies sound like wonderful places to work!

You will have to pardon the skepticism, but you need to carefully dissect any ad before responding. In many cases, what is stated in the ad may not align with reality. To re-affirm that point, read an ad placed by one of your previous employers and after allowing for a potential tainted viewpoint, pose the question: "Is this a proper reflection of what this company really stands for?"

On the plus side, a well-prepared and honest career ad can supply you with a great deal of valuable information. A good ad should be designed to facilitate the pre-screening process and it should be directed at only those who qualify for the position in question. Unfortunately, not all ads fall in this category and you may need to do a little additional research before deciding if it is truly worthwhile to respond. From the company's standpoint, a good career ad should convey most, if not all of the following:

- Who we are and how great we are
- Our culture and our vision
- What we must have in terms of credentials
- What we would like to have
- Possibly salary / benefit information
- Advancement opportunities
- Job location and / or mobility factors
- Details

     - Send to... using reference #...
     - Possible fax number
     - Response times
     - How you will be kept informed

Company Process

You have no control over how the company will handle the processing of incoming letters and resumes. Companies can collect all the envelopes for a week before sitting down to start the review process. They can rough sort each day's incoming mail, they can have several people screening the mail by using a pre-qualifier template or you might find one person who is assigned the task of sorting and deciding if your correspondence initially goes in:

"The Keeper Pile"   **"The Maybe Stack"**   **"The Reject Bin"**

Frankly, the best method for the company is to have one person doing all the pre-screening, all at one time. This improves consistency. Regardless of the system, you want to make it easy for the initial reviewer and you want to make a favourable impression before they even turn the page to look at your resume.

Analyzing and Responding to the Ad

Armed with all that background information, just how do you go about responding to an ad and how do you get in the "Keeper" or "Maybe" pile to ultimately secure that critical interview?

The best way to work though this process is with a live example in front of you which represents a position you are considering. Read the ad two or three times and then transcribe the information on to a separate piece of paper using a format which is similar to the Career Ad Analyzer, as illustrated in the Appendix - Graphics & Forms # 5. This may appear to be an unnecessary step but un-cluttering the available data by removing it from the ad format can prove helpful.

If you want to save some time, immediately move to the "Critical Requirements" and the "Preferred Requirements" section. As you read and re-read the ad, jot down what the company wants and/or would like to have. The format in the ad analyzer highlights the categories which most often appear but there may be additional criteria which you can insert under the "Other" heading.

Once you have completed this exercise, you will have a clear understanding of what the company wants. The next challenge is for you to honestly look at each requirement to determine if you have the right credentials. There are no magic formulas but common sense dictates you had best have most of the "Critical Requirements" and some of the "Preferred Requirements" if you want to be a serious contender.

If you are comfortable about applying for the position, fill out the balance of the ad analyzer. The company background information section is included to assist you in pulling out key words and phrases which will give you a feel for the organization. How do they work, what is their focus, what type of language do they use, and generally what do they view as being important. All this information is helpful in terms of eventually preparing a letter which identifies their stated criteria and aligns those requirements with your strengths, supported by your tangible accomplishments.

The chapter on letter writing covers many issues which have applicability to correspondence in response to career ads. A large number of people responding to career ads take the easy route and simply say they have seen the ad, they are qualified as per the attached resume and they look forward to hearing from the company.

Adopting this approach does not set you apart from your host of competitors! Conversely, the correspondence suggested in the Appendix - Sample Letters # 11 immediately catches the attention of the reader because you have expended the time to identify those key requirements of the advertised position and you have clearly delineated why you meet and/or exceed the specification of the job. Again, you have capitalized on an opportunity to highlight why you stand out from the masses.

Make it Easy for the Reviewer or Decision Maker

As stated before, you have no idea about the mechanical sorting and selection process used by a company. As such, you want to ensure that your entire presentation is impressive. Do not assume no one will look at the envelope. For all you know, the reviewer could open every envelope, peruse your letter and quickly scan your resume before categorizing your acceptability for closer scrutiny. You can leave nothing to chance and a properly presented envelope might be as important as your letter.

In the initial sorting process, your letter must grab the reviewer's attention. If it does not, they may never get as far as your fantastic resume. Format and presentation are dealt with in the letter writing chapter but what you want to accomplish is to get the reviewer's head nodding up and down, in agreement with what you have said.

If you have carefully extracted and highlighted their key requirements the reader naturally and immediately senses you understand the job specifications.

By crisply noting your strengths and skills, supported by quantifiable examples, the reviewer is again inclined to be positive about your submission. A reviewer faced with the task of looking at a couple of hundred letters, or more, does not take kindly to flipping back and forth through your material in an effort to determine if you have the basic qualifications. If a reviewer is forced to expend too much time and effort, you might be hearing from the company far more quickly than you would like.

Throughout the letter your goal should be to sustain the reviewer's positive head nodding. Do not confuse the issue by using alternate terminology. Repeat the phrases that appear in the ad. In all likelihood, this is the verbiage commonly used by the company. If the ad says "bottom line driven" do not utilize the phrase "profit orientation" in your covering letter. Give the reviewer a sense that you are in sync with the company.

Follow-Up

At the beginning of this chapter the expression "See It! Send It! Sit Back & Wait!" was quoted. Hopefully, the preceding pages have assisted you in deciding if you should reply and how your response should be presented. But how do you go about enhancing your chances to be selected for the all important interview?

Like everything else in the job search, ads need to be followed-up with some additional activity on your part. Sitting back and waiting is not the suggested course of action. While company recruiters may want to tear out the next few pages, you can improve your chances for an interview through a proper follow-up by phone. If a phone number has not been recorded in the ad (most do not) you will need to do a little extra detective work. The purpose behind the follow-up is not to become a pest but to accentuate your keen desire to progress to the next phase - the interview.

The other critical detail to remember is that the name or position quoted as the reference in the ad is not necessarily the final decision maker. There is apt to be a line manager out there in the system somewhere who is simply waiting for a short list of potential candidates to arrive on his or her desk.

Let me give you some sample dialogue which you might use in follow-up scenarios. Just for the sake of argument, let's start with the receptionist in a Human Resources Department who has been receiving thirty calls a day about a recently run ad. Does that give you your first clue? Give the receptionist time for a coffee, but make your call during the first half hour of business.

Receptionist: *"Good morning, this is Ann in Human Resources. May I help you?"*

Ray: *"Hi Ann, this is Ray Price calling. I was hoping you might be able to assist me."*

Ann: *"Sure, what can I do for you?"*

Ray: *"I responded to the ad concerning the position of ___ two weeks ago. I realize you were likely flooded with replies but I wanted to get some sense about the process your company normally uses when you run an ad. Can you help me or can you refer me to the right person?"*

Ann: *"Well, the person handling the recruitment for that area is Mary Jones but she is unable to accept any calls because of the high volumes you mentioned earlier."*

Ray: *"I appreciate her situation but perhaps you could answer one or two general questions. Can you tell me who will be selecting the interview finalists - would it be Ms. Jones or the actual manager of the area involved and have they targeted a firm date to start the interview process?"*

Ann: *"I think they are both involved but I don't believe they will select finalists for a couple more weeks."*

Ray: *"And could you tell me who the line manager might be or at least the name of the department that has the opening?"*

Ann: *"Well, I don't know the name of the manager but it is in our _____ department."*

This dialogue could go on for the rest of the book but suffice to say through polite and probing questions, you can gather more information - all aimed at providing yourself with an edge. If you do get through to the person who is presumably responsible for the pre-selection process, you want to politely pose a few more questions such as:

"I appreciate you have had a number of responses but I wanted to express my keen interest in the position. I was also wondering about your selection criteria for setting up interviews and when those meetings may take place."

"Would you be handling the final selection process directly or might there be some line managers involved? I recognize your time is limited, thank you for the additional information and I look forward to hearing from you in the near future."

By making a favourable impression on the phone, the chances of the reviewer remembering you in a positive light may work to your advantage the next time they are perusing the letters and resumes, preparatory to deciding on the short list or the interview list. If you have been able to ascertain the name of the final decision maker, you have some options to weigh and consider.

1. If you have another contact within the company, you may wish to reconnect to discuss the feasibility of having them send a copy of your resume to the decision maker.

2. If you do not have a contact, you might simply write the decision maker directly, indicating it has come to your attention that the company may have a vacancy and you would be interested in discussing your candidacy. In essence, you are tackling the situation on two fronts.

    There is little downside risk to this move. If you are already on the short-list, the decision maker has seen or heard your name twice. If you have done a good job in presenting yourself, you have likely enhanced your opportunities.

    Managers usually like to think they know more about hiring than the people in Human Resource Departments. Do not be a pest but remember that persistence and perseverance are qualities that most managers admire.

3. You might even approach the decision maker purely on the basis of wanting to network.

Again, the whole purpose in follow-up is to put your name forward in a positive light and to set yourself apart from all the others who have applied. Take a minute and re-read Calvin Coolidge's remarks about persistence.

Responding to career ads can have several advantages over and above the primary objective of securing the position in question.

You have an opportunity to sharpen your writing skills, you can gather additional information about a prospective employer and above all else, you can indirectly expand your network by showcasing yourself to people who are in positions of influence. By dedicating a proper portion of your time and effort to career ads, you will be positively advancing your job search.

"Character is the result of two things - mental

attitude and the way we spend our time."

- Elbert Hubbard

Chapter 13

THE INTERVIEW

The subject of interviewing has been done, re-done and done again. Unfortunately, if you speak with recruiters and interviewers, they will soon tell you that people continue to repeat the same old mistakes which cause qualified candidates to get edged out by a competitor.

So before launching headlong into proper interviewing techniques, let me try to make a point which will hopefully cause you to reflect on every piece of advice that follows. For the sake of argument, let us carry through with the scenario we painted in the last chapter where you have responded to an ad. If it had national coverage there were likely upwards to 500 replies and assume you have secured a first interview.

Even if the company were interviewing 50 possibles, which is unlikely, you have made it into the top 10%. In short, your qualifications are not a major issue or you would not be using up valuable interviewing time. So what makes the difference when it comes to the final selection? You've got it - the interview!

Just a side note, coming in as a strong second or third can have some advantages as well, if you have been so impressive that the company would genuinely like to work you into another part of their team. In such situations, you will want to follow-through with some very active post reject letter networking (See Appendix - Sample Letter - # 14).

Turn back to one of the first pages in this book. What do you see?

Focus - Organization - Research - Activity

Those four words are as crucial in the interview process as they are in any other part of the job search.

When focusing is mentioned in conjunction with interviewing, the most common response from an individual is that they are well focused and they know precisely what direction they want to head with their career. You can not argue the response but if you have a focus as it pertains to interviewing, direct your initial attention to the image you portray.

Sound like another boring cliché? Well perhaps it is but based on my personal experiences as an interviewer and judging from comments made by recruitment specialists, a host of potential candidates are not paying attention to the basics of putting forth a good image. There are three components to image: How you look. What you do. What you say.

How You Look

Given previous statements about people still not taking heed of the volumes written on "How To" prepare from an image standpoint, a last valiant attempt will be made to stress some critical points. Bear in mind, this book is directed toward middle managers who are seeking fairly traditional work situations. As such, the following few pages concerning image are not intended for the budding rock star or a trendy fashion model. Perhaps reversing the approach might have a greater impact!

How to Dress for the Unsuccessful Interview!

Men, don't:
- visit your barber on a regular basis
- attend to those ill fitting or out of date glasses
- ease up on the after shave - apply it liberally
- have your interview shirts professionally laundered
- bother to have your suits meticulously cleaned
- invest in a couple of "middle of the road" silk ties
- bother to adjust your tie squarely before the interview
- worry about the small grease spot on the tie
- wear a good quality leather belt
- concern yourself with a manicure check
- give a second thought to wearing ankle length socks
- buff and polish your shoes before every interview
- think twice about carrying a cheap looking pen
- give a fleeting thought to cleaning up the old briefcase

Ladies, do:
- select an uncomplimentary hair style
- wear your rattiest pair of glasses
- buy and apply perfume in large doses
- insist on wearing garish jewelry
- select a party type ensemble
- bedeck each finger with a ring or two
- wear only blouses which have not been properly pressed
- choose nylons with a run
- forget to carry an extra pair of nylons
- accessorize with scuffed shoes
- carry a worn handbag
- bring along a "monster" bag instead of a briefcase

The negative approach may be somewhat flippant but it is so important to realize the huge and instantaneous impact created by physical image. It is not a matter of being beautiful or handsome but it is a matter of being well turned out. Over and above that, you should always err on the side of being conservative and dress like you would if you were attending the most formal of business meetings. And, use common sense!

What You Do

Having created a good visual first impression with an interviewer, your task is far from complete. Indeed, it begins again, a fraction of a second after the interviewer has clamped eyes on you for the first time. There are obviously several other points to ponder in the whole interviewing process but like selecting proper attire, the issue comes back to common sense and the basics. The following items are intended to give you some straight forward hints.

What You Do - The Smile

From the time we were infants this most simplistic of facial expressions has been flaunted as being some miracle elixir. "Smile and the world smiles with you." "A frown is nothing but a smile upside down." We have all been conned into smiling for the camera, from toddler-hood to adulthood. Every marketing or sales seminar you ever attended would have extolled the virtues of a smile. And you know, they are right! There is nothing more engaging than having someone greet you with a smile. That simple muscular movement can truly set the stage for a pleasant exchange during an interview.

What You Do - The Hand Shake

Like dressing for success and smiling, volumes have been written on the intricacies and meanings of various hand shaking styles.

Most of us have read about the right way and the wrong way to shake hands but the truth be told, all those words of wisdom seem to disappear when an interviewer thrusts his or her hand forward.

Do not minimize the importance of a good hand shake because it likely comes in as a close second to a confident smile. If you want to spend a great deal of time perfecting the hand shake, do some research on the subject. My advice is simple. Hand shakes should be firmly confident but not bone crushing and the duration should be short. You are not pumping for water. We are all human and most people will overlook hand shaking shortcomings, other than the "limp wristed" exchange and that applies to both men and women. If you fall in the latter category, fix it!

What You Do - Confidence

It is only natural to be anxious or apprehensive going into an interview situation but you are there for a reason. You have been selected as a finalist. If your confidence starts to crumble as you prepare for an interview, just reflect back on what you have done to get to that stage. You have focused yourself on a clear career objective, you have run an organized campaign, you have re-searched the company and you have actively pursued your goals.

You have every right to be confident. Just make certain you do not step over the fine line which will cause you to be seen as arrogant, egotistical and overbearing. Establish an air of confidence via your winning smile, a business like hand shake and a confident walk. Carry the theme through by being friendly, personable and by demonstrating that you are comfortable with yourself.

Your personal confidence can be further accentuated by regularly referring to the interviewer by name. Similarly, maintaining eye contact can be extremely important to demonstrate your alertness and genuine interest in what is being discussed.

What You Do - Posture and Animation

Generally speaking, people have difficulty in controlling mannerisms which have been developed over a lifetime. This is very evident in terms of personal posture and gesturing. If you are concentrating all your thought resources on how you are sitting and whether or not your hand/arms are moving about, you are apt to be so engrossed in worrying about these issues that you will not respond effectively to the questions being posed.

The middle of the road is the best approach and most of us can make a sufficient number of personal adjustments to accomplish the needed degree of change. Ramrod straight posture suggests a high level of anxiety and on the other hand, slouching might indicate a lack of interest. Strike a happy medium. Be relaxed but attentive and alert.

Some of us tend to be over animated and too much hand gesturing can be distracting or disconcerting to an interviewer. Those of us who fall in this category know who we are and if you are uncertain, ask a friend or close relative.

The best method to cut down on exaggerated and constant hand language is simply to keep your hands together. The pose, if you will, looks comfortable and you can easily catch yourself before over accentuating your words. Some gesturing is good, it can demonstrate your enthusiasm and passion for topics.

What You Say

To this point, we have covered image and things you can do to put forward a good impression. Now let's concentrate on what you convey through speaking.

What You Say - Voice and Speaking

If you have occasion to ask interviewers or recruiters about their most dreaded sessions, the soft-spoken monotone speaker will be very high on the list. From personal experience, your entire energy level is concentrated on listening or staying awake.

It is a pleasure to interview someone who can naturally vary the pitch and tone of their voice to demonstrate their excitement and enthusiasm. Similarly, it is reassuring to an interviewer if candidates periodically pause to take the time to reflect on questions or to gather their thoughts before responding. Constant staccato retorts can be a sign of overly rehearsed replies.

Speech intensity (volume) and rate are two other factors which you need to consider. As noted earlier, the constantly quiet-spoken person can be a real distraction but conversely, the shouter can be equally annoying. The fast talker or slow drawler can also grate on the nerves of the most patient interviewer.

Above all else, be natural. An interviewer will definitely be much more impressed by a straight-forward, unaffected conversation than by the dialogue which is peppered with incorrect phrases that are obviously not part of your daily vocabulary. It goes without saying that either gender should not lapse into "locker room" language.

If you have a habit of using one or two favorite phrases with great frequency, like "yup" or a host of like expressions, try to wean yourself off these repetitive words.

With this ever lengthening list of things to do and things not to do, people often ask how they can possibly remember all these subtle nuances. Making the necessary alterations cannot be done the night before an interview. That is one of the big pluses to networking meetings. While you are out gathering information and moving your job search forward, you are automatically providing yourself with an opportunity to refine your interviewing skills, in an non-interviewing environment.

If you begin to develop and hone your interviewing skills at the beginning of the networking process, you will be amazed at how well you have prepared yourself for the first real interview.

What You Say - Twelve Illusive Questions

Interviewing would be great if everyone played fair and asked all the same questions in the same order. But no one ever used the word fair in a sentence relating to the interview process.

Life would be simple if you had a list of the interview questions and better still, if this book could give you the pat answers. Not so. Indeed, even if the questions were common knowledge, the responses have to come from you, in your own words and in your individual style. What can be done is to generalize about the more common questions and give you background rationale which will assist you in formulating answers designed to set you apart from the competitors.

These are in no particular order and in fact, not all the questions may even be posed. However, there is a very reasonable chance that the interviewer will attempt to ascertain your views on most of these issues. You have a personal responsibility to prepare yourself for every possible inquiry.

1.   Tell me a little bit about yourself.

2.   What were the circumstances surrounding your departure from your last employer?

3.   Please summarize your work history.

4.   We all have strengths and weaknesses. What are your major strengths and weaknesses?

5.   Explain why you are pursuing career opportunities in our industry?

6.   What do you know about our company and why do you want to work for us?

7.   If you could choose a boss, what would they be like and how would you describe them?

8.   Would you explain why you are qualified for this position and why we should select you?

9.   What are your five year career goals and what factors do you see influencing your achievement of these personal objectives?

10.   What questions can I answer for you?

11.   Let me pose a hypothetical situation. I would be interested in how you would handle the situation.

12.   What are your salary expectations?

Illusive questions? Perhaps. If you have taken the time to formulate points which will address these and similar queries, your replies will be well thought out and at the same time spontaneous. Thorough preparation will also assist you in avoiding rambling answers which can be as distracting to an interviewer as the monotone speaker.

Gone are the days of singular questions and responses. Interviewers want to garner some sense about how you think on your feet and many of the questions are double or triple barreled.

Your real challenge is not simply answering the questions but you want to anticipate the subsequent question. One of the most effective means of ensuring that you answer properly is to listen carefully to the question itself and when necessary, do not hesitate to clarify before responding.

Your replies should be concise but where applicable, you will want to expand just enough to minimize further probing inquiries on a particular subject. But avoid rambling. It is like responding to a career ad. Make it easy for the interviewer. Wherever possible, illustrate your reply with a quantifiable example where you can highlight your accomplishments or strengths. Above all else, be truthful and always maintain a positive attitude.

Pre-Interview

At some point, you will receive your first call asking you to come in for an interview. Most everyone will admit you are so busy concentrating on who, when and where, that you rarely ask any other questions. But if you are prepared and if you have your wits about you, it is important to make other inquiries before hanging up.

If a search firm is involved, they will generally relay a great deal of information to you. On the other hand, if you have secured the interview yourself, you might pose some or all of the following queries to the individual who has phoned to set up a time. This person could be the actual interviewer or it might be someone just making the arrangements.

> *"Can you tell me who will be conducting the interview and what position they hold with your company?"*

> *"Can you tell me what type of interview format you use (structured, unstructured, one-on-one, panel)?"*

> *"The ad was fairly generic, could you provide me with some additional specifics about the job, such as the responsibilities and reporting lines?"*

Many interviews will arise from networking situations and in such cases, asking for more information is considerably easier because in one fashion or another, you have already established a rapport with either the interviewer or with someone who is known to the caller.

Be prepared for those interviews where your networking has paid off but where the company may not have a particular job in mind. Such interviews are usually informal and general, but nonetheless very important.

If you have been faithfully following the pre-meeting research suggested in Chapter Ten, you will be very comfortable about doing the background work required prior to the actual interview. Now you can really zero-in on information which may position you to set yourself apart from the other competitors.

Clearly, your focus will depend on the type of position in question and the company. Over and above what you can glean from recent media coverage, you will likely want to give some thought to:

- Historical profit performance
- Future company directions or strategies
- Working environment
    - Conservative / structured
    - Aggressive / freewheeling
    - Paternalistic
- Career growth opportunities
- Range of products and services
- Reputation in the market

Having already spent time becoming conversant with some of the stock questions, review your interview notes. It is useless to memorize responses verbatim because even commonly asked questions are phrased in a variety of ways. You simply want to keep the highlights in your mind to allow yourself to reply spontaneously but not in a contrived manner.

Remember, your replies must be honest and you want to convey a positive attitude, both by your spoken words and in your overall mannerisms. Depending upon your own level of confidence, you might want to try some responses out loud or even into a tape recorder. You will also want to carefully review your resume.

Take along an extra copy of your resume and copies of important credentials, such as academic confirmations. Similarly, have your references typed on a separate sheet of paper, including all addresses and phone numbers. The balance of your pre-interview preparation is almost identical to the steps we discussed when getting ready for a networking meeting.

The Interview

You are not a "hat-in-hand street urchin" asking for a menial factory job at the turn of the 19th century. To get to the interview stage, you have already impressed several people with your credentials, your background and your approach.

Normally, the first interview will concentrate on four major issues:

1.   Overall image
2.   Capability and willingness to do the job
3.   Fit with the employer
4.   Assessment of the risk associated with hiring you

We have already covered the subject of image. These days, more and more interviewers are immediately moving toward issues of "fit". By heavily concentrating on this area, questions about capabilities and willingness will virtually be answered automatically. A good interviewer can satisfy concerns about technical proficiencies by posing multiple questions such as: "What are your opinions about company sponsored outside training for employees and how would you go about developing your team if they were all asked to convert to the "xyz" program within six months?"

In essence, you have been asked three questions. The first two segments are quite standard but the last part about the specific program is likely included to garner some feel for your technical knowledge - assuming of course it is a requirement of the job. In a similar vein, responses to "fit" questions will either diminish or accentuate the potential risk associated with hiring you.

Many people make the mistake of assuming an interview is solely dedicated to putting forth your answers to questions. On the surface that may appear to be true but you also have a responsibility to the interviewer and yourself to listen carefully and where necessary to clarify what is being asked. It is not an interviewing sin to admit you have not grasped a question and it is infinitely better to clarify matters rather than responding incorrectly.

The average first interview lasts approximately one hour from introduction to the final hand shake. Shorter interviews are not uncommon and duration is not necessarily a measure of interest or disinterest. After you have a few interviews under your belt, you will be able to sense how well they have gone.

If you take the time to analyze what transpires during a one hour interview, perhaps you will be more at ease. Automatically, the first ten minutes are spent in introductions and generally building some degree of rapport, on both sides. The last five minutes are dedicated to summing up. That leaves a scant 45 minutes for questions and answers. For the sake of argument, divide the 45 minutes by the 12 questions we used as examples and you are down to about 4 minutes per question and reply.

Of course it is never that cut and dry but this will give you some idea about how much "air time" you have to fill and on average it works out to 30 minutes. If you look back on the points you have prepared in response to the 12 illusive questions, you will soon discover you have more than enough good material to cover your portion of the one hour. In fact, you will find the biggest challenge is not answering the questions but answering them in a manner which will allow you to best showcase all your positives.

The interviewer will control the length of the meeting and the wind-up will be quite evident. Normally, he or she will say something like: "We have covered a great deal of information today and I appreciate you taking the time to come in for this meeting. Do you have any final questions?" Most of us are so pleased with ourselves, having made it through the interview, there is a tendency to say "No, I don't believe I have any other questions. Thank you for taking the time to see me."

The above dialogue is polite but it is also common place. If you want to set yourself apart from your competitors, you will fine tune a strong finish. While it is important to avoid canned commentaries, your closing remarks can be a little more rehearsed because in the majority of cases, you know you will be given the opportunity to say a few final words. In a well-prepared close, you want to quickly accomplish the following:

- Acknowledge the interviewer's expertise
- Re-affirm your keen interest
- Garner feed back
- Determine the next step
- Stay in control
- Thank the interviewer

Please, please script your own thoughts and words or interviewers and recruiters will ban this book! However, the following example illustrates a strong closing statement to the final question:

> *"I don't believe I have any specific questions about the position or your company. Your information was very comprehensive and your questions gave me the opportunity to address the issues which I felt were important to convey.*
>
> *Having heard more about the position and your organization, I would like to stress I am keenly interested in progressing our discussions further. Can you give me an initial sense of how well my qualifications and interests match with your expectations and what might be the next step in your selection process?"*

Unless you have completely blown the interview, the response to your inquiries is apt to be positive or at the very least, non committal. But, you have demonstrated your interest, desire and just enough assertiveness. If the interviewer is quite specific in terms of the time frames, do not press the issue but if the reply is vague, attempt to re-establish control. Sum up with a thank you and do not linger. Interviewers like to keep to their predetermined schedules and you do not want to be remembered as the person who eliminated the only coffee break of the afternoon.

After the Interview

In the vast majority of cases, one interview will not result in a job offer. With this in mind, it is important to start preparing for the second encounter as soon as you have concluded the first meeting.

While things are still fresh in your memory, sit down and recap what you have learned about the position and the company. Then jot down the questions which were posed and highlight your own responses. Thinking about the entire interview, evaluate yourself in terms of where you did well and where you need to improve. This self-assessment will be important for the second interview or for interviews with other companies.

Write all this information down! Interviewers keep records and when you go back for a second or even a third interview, you want to be consistent. You can imagine the disastrous results if you keep changing your comments about your strengths and weaknesses. Then follow-up in writing to thank the interviewer and again re-enforce your high interest level. No, this is not seen as grovelling! Indeed, you are once again demonstrating your attention to detail and your professional courtesy. What is even more important, you are setting yourself apart from others.

The Second Interview

Second interviews trigger personal responses which can range from the euphoria of being on the last "short-list" to the nagging fear of how you will feel if you do not get an offer. In either case, it is timely to remind yourself you have reached this plateau by following the basics of running a focused, organized, well-researched and active job search campaign. Do not let up now!

Return to the notes you made after the first interview. Take what you learned about the company and the position and thread that information into the highlights you use to respond to the twelve common questions. By doing so, you will significantly bolster your presentation and you will be in better position to deal with new hypothetical questions which are geared to potential or real situations within the company.

Do not be put off by repeat questions which are identical to the ones used in the last meeting. Remember, you are likely to be facing a new interviewer for the second interview and they want to hear your responses to stock questions which the company uses.

Be consistent and take the opportunity to further enhance your good replies. If you felt you explained something poorly in the first interview, now is your chance to make amends.

The balance of the procedure is identical to the first interview. The one exception might be the discussions about the next step, simply because all parties concerned recognize that a decision is close at hand. Actually it is not uncommon to have a verbal offer tabled and this aspect will be addressed in the negotiating section.

The Telephone Interview

Telephone interviews always come out of left field and as such, it is important to keep organized at your home office. Sometimes these conversations start off as innocent calls to clarify a few details and they end up being mini, non face-to-face interviews. As such, the safest route is to automatically treat these calls as telephone interviews.

Telephone pre-screening or phone interviews are becoming much more common place and they can put you at a real disadvantage because you do not have time to prepare. However, if you have been organized enough to outline the salient responses in advance, you will have re-gained the advantage.

Pity the poor individual who receives a pre-screening call and has always assumed they would have time to formulate responses the night before an interview!

Depending upon the circumstances, your follow-up to a telephone interview can be exactly the same as what you would do after a live situation.

Negotiating

There it is! An offer for a position which is ideally suited to you. Do you grab it and run, or do you negotiate?

The first thing to remember is most companies have expended a considerable amount of time and energy in arriving at the decision to make you an offer. Number two, they want you and at least notionally, if they do not secure your services they will need to revert to the second choice. And third, the vast majority of companies expect some degree of negotiating.

Most offers record an acceptance deadline and now is not the time for you to start checking the market to determine if the terms and conditions of the offer are in line with industry norms. Getting a sense about total compensation packages for your area of interest is something you want to accomplish during your various networking sessions.

When you are at the point of being given an offer, ensure you understand the entire remuneration package, including benefits and perks. A healthy looking base salary may not be nearly as attractive if you are responsible for many of your own benefits. Even seemingly nice perks like cars can have considerable negative complications which will erode your base salary when tax time arrives.

When dealing with various non-salary items (vacation entitlements, parking, waiting periods for benefits) you need to negotiate these before you become an employee. You could be in for a rude surprise if you concede to the comment: "Don't worry about those minor details, we'll work all that out when you arrive." Once you are on board, you are an employee and you are subject to company rules and regulations. All too often, line managers make well-meaning commitments, only to find the company has unbendable policies.

In terms of salary negotiations, you have a couple of options. Clearly you want to maximize your starting salary but if negotiations begin to sputter in this area, be prepared with a rational back-up position. If you cannot achieve the exact salary you have in mind, be flexible. Table the idea of an automatic increase in three or six months, conditional upon you demonstrating your worth to the company. You get what you want in a reasonably short period of time and the company feels more comfortable because they can tie their dollars to tested performance.

In all these situations, have absolutely every detail outlined in the final written offer. It is not a matter of not trusting one another, it is simply good business practice to be precise in any contractual undertaking. If incentive compensation forms part of your overall package, have this information clearly spelled out in the offer or alternatively ensure you have a copy of the company's incentive compensation program.

Interviewing and negotiating can either be nerve racking or fun. The choice is really up to you. If you insist upon running an ad hoc job search campaign, these two experiences are apt to be less than pleasant. On the other hand, if you constantly reflect on Focus, Organization, Research and Activity, you are much more likely to truly enjoy interviewing for your ideal position and negotiating a fair compensation package.

"If you want work well done, select a busy man

- the other kind has no time."

                                        - Elbert Hubbard

Chapter 14

LETTER WRITING

Throughout this book, the prime importance of written communications has be stressed and re-stressed.

Many ask us why this seemingly antiquated method of communication is still accentuated! Can we not convey our messages via short notes, on the fax machine, through carefully developed resumes or structured commentaries on voice mail? The answer is quite simple. If you want to stand out from your competitors who are also attempting to tap the hidden job market, well written letters can aid significantly in this process.

Your goal is to set yourself apart from others! An informal, yet professionally crafted letter can do just that - regardless of the type of job you are seeking. Grasp the opportunity to communicate in writing and position yourself to be on the leading edge - well out in front of the others.

In the Appendix, you will find models of several letters which respond to typical situations but for you to effectively convert these samples for your own use, it is important to understand some basic letter writing principles. In essence, when it comes to letter writing you need to be cognizant of two primary items, those being presentation and organization.

Presentation

Under the general heading of presentation, we will look at certain major components which are all important if you are to make a favourable impact on the recipient of your letters. These are common sense items but they are worth reviewing to ensure you achieve maximum value from every piece of correspondence you dispatch.

Presentation - Impression

Not unlike the first impression you make when meeting someone, your letters do exactly the same thing. With this in mind, you really have to start with the messenger of your letter, the envelope.

Detail is a major factor and the address itself must be completely accurate and typed, with the individual addressee clearly identified. If you are sending enclosures, you should definitely be using a large envelope to avoid the unnecessary folding of material.

The letter itself must be produced on premium paper, it should be formatted in a business-like fashion and the print quality (whether typed or word processed) should be absolutely superior.

Presentation - Accuracy

All too often, people write great letters but simple errors and omissions significantly detract from what otherwise may be an outstanding piece of correspondence.

It goes without saying that spelling and grammar must be checked meticulously but you should also be alert to other factors which could be construed as sensitive issues to the recipient. In these rapidly changing times, companies are often faced with name changes brought about by mergers and acquisitions. Make certain you are using the exact name of the company, including proper punctuation and abbreviations.

Similarly, companies can have several locations and you want to double check that your letter is going to reach the recipient at his or her specific office. You do not want someone thinking to themselves: "They didn't even take the time to find out my proper address!"

The same care is required in verifying the current title of the person who will receive your letter. Titles change and many people are extremely sensitive about their official ranking within their organization. Remember, it denotes their position and stature in the company and in many cases they have earned the designation through a great deal of personal effort. Show your respect by taking the time to get the title correct.

Presentation - Style

Style is a very important aspect of good letter writing and there are a number of features that come into play, not the least of which is your personal written mannerism. Remember, if you try to mimic someone else, it will quickly become very evident that you are not the true author of your correspondence. Worst still, this will become even more noticeable during a face-to-face meeting. So be yourself when you write, but also incorporate the methodologies noted in this material.

Over and above "personalizing" your letters, there are other issues which you want to consider in terms of overall style. It is important to accent your own professionalism by conveying your thoughts in an honest and forthright fashion.

Letter length is also a factor to keep in mind. While it is important to relay your full message, it is also critical that you respect the time limitations of the recipient. Time is one of the most precious commodities in the business world and you should always acknowledge that reality in your correspondence.

Presentation - Jargon

Industries, companies and organizations have always developed and used their own jargon but in the past ten years, the lexicon of words and phrases has mushroomed. Properly using jargon in your letters can be a very powerful means of demonstrating your familiarity with the business in question.

Conversely, using incorrect and/or outdated business terminology can illustrate that you have not been keeping pace in an ever changing work environment. If you are going to use jargon, use it sparingly and take the time to make certain you are up to date on current phrases.

Presentation - Future Dialogue

During your job search, almost every letter writing situation should be focused on expanding your network and progressing your relationship with the recipient of your correspondence. Indeed, in most scenarios, you are attempting to position yourself to tap into other valuable contacts and connections.

Some of the best letter writers fail to "leave the door ajar" for future opportunities to either correspond, verbally communicate or perhaps to meet the person in question. It is crucial that your letters specifically address this issue, thereby allowing you to naturally reconnect with your contacts at the appropriate times throughout your job search.

Organization

In almost every work scenario, considerable emphasis is placed upon the ability to be organized and to get things done in a logical and orderly fashion. If organization is extremely important in day-to-day business activities, it becomes critical when you are searching for a new career.

By extension, organization is also a key factor in both written communications and the subsequent steps which will ultimately flow from your correspondence.

Organization - Referencing

As noted at the outset, one of the reasons behind letter writing is to allow you to effectively *showcase* yourself to potential employers and to others who might be in a position to assist you in your job search.

In the vast majority of cases, people who receive your letters will be favourably impressed if you accurately record names, dates, places and situations. This attention to detail says something about you as an individual and as a prospective working associate. Take a look at a few examples:

1.   "John Smith, the Director of Research at_____ suggested I should give you a call...." is certainly better than "John Smith suggested I call you about...."

      The recipient of this particular letter may know four "John Smith's".

2.   "I simply wanted to thank you for seeing me on the 1st of June." is better than "I simply wanted to thank you for seeing me."

        Specifying dates accentuates your attention to organization and detail.

3.   "Your comments about the construction of a new facility in Surrey, B.C. were...." is better than "Your comments about the construction of a new facility in the Vancouver area were...."

        Quoting specifics denotes that you were carefully listening during the conversation.

4.   "During our conversation you mentioned a new initiative known as **Quality 2000**..." is much better than "During our conversation you talked about dealing with some service quality issues in the future...."

        Again, you demonstrate that you were paying close attention to the details of the conversation.

Organization - Research

One of the corner stones of running a good job search campaign is research. Proper research can also enhance your written communication skills, often setting you apart from others. Research can be as simple as taking the time to verify the proper company name, address and title of the person who will receive your letter.

Once you have established a rapport with an individual, you will want to identify various ways and means of maintaining and cultivating that relationship over the long-term. As illustrated in the Appendix - Sample Letters # 4, this can be accomplished by reconnecting and forwarding material which speaks to topical items of joint interest.

To do this, you must maintain sufficient notes about previous meetings and/or phone conversations. All of this requires that you keep abreast of information - including sources like the newspapers, periodicals, trade journals, annual reports and annual meetings.

Constantly reading and researching will allow you to initiate contact with a good prospect or to maintain a relationship which you have already begun to develop.

Organization - Follow Up

Timeliness of follow-up is perhaps one of the best means of demonstrating you possess a trait which is highly regarded in the business world. In the examples provided in the Appendix, most of the letters either spell out precisely when you will reconnect or they suggest what circumstances will cause you to re-establish contact. If you have set a specific time to follow-up with a person, you must ensure you meet that commitment. In those cases where you have generalized about follow-up, weigh and consider the best timing and do it!

Maintaining the written portion of your job search campaign requires personal dedication and it can not be done in a haphazard fashion. If you do not enjoy writing, it is very easy to become distracted and thoughts such as some of those recorded below can easily cause the written portion of the job search process to sputter and stall.

"I've already written this person twice in the past three months...."

"It probably wouldn't make any difference...."

"I sent some great information and didn't even receive a thank you...."

"I haven't got time, I've got some other good prospects in the wings...."

"I will do it later...."

Successful job seekers diligently maintain their written communications and above all else, they start to self-manage their ongoing careers by writing the "last letter" - the one informing your **new** network about successfully starting your **new** career.

With all this background information in mind, carefully review the letters in the Appendix of this book. The samples not only deal with common scenarios but also some less traditional approaches.

Chapter 15

NEW HORIZONS

Life has always been punctuated with highs and lows. Sometimes events impact solely upon you but more often than not, circumstances will also touch your family and friends.

If the loss of a job is a low, I can say without reservation that successfully securing a new and meaningful position is one of the ultimate highs. It is quite natural to enthusiastically share the great news with your loved ones and close friends.

After you have celebrated your new found career, take a moment to reflect on what you have learned and accomplished. If nothing else, you have had to critically analyze who you are, what you are good at and how you want to balance your career and your personal life. Do not get so caught up in your new work that you lose sight of what you have discovered.

On the surface, your most significant accomplishment may seem to be landing a new job. Indeed, if you have truly subscribed to the philosophy of networking, you have accomplished even more. Remember, networking is not just a process - it is a state of mind.

Start the ongoing maintenance of your network today by corresponding with everyone who has supported and sponsored you during your job search. They deserve to know you have successfully landed.

If you continue to maintain and expand your network, you will find your day-to-day job satisfaction will increase and you will prosper and grow in your new business surroundings.

Good luck and every success in your future endeavours!

APPENDIX

SAMPLE LETTERS

REQUEST FOR A NETWORKING MEETING

REFERENCING AN ASSOCIATE

ABC COMPANY INC.
1235 - WEST STREET
SOMEWHERE, CANADA L4G 1N2

June 20th, 199_

Attention: Mr. Bill Smith, Director of Marketing

Dear Bill,

First let me introduce myself as we have not met but during a recent discussion with John Jones, the Director of Product Marketing at YYZ Company, he suggested I should make an effort to contact you.

Just by way of a brief background, I have spent the past 10 years in the _____ industry and I am currently seeking new career options. Let me stress, I am not looking for a position with your organization but John felt your expertise would be of considerable assistance in terms of the job market research which I am presently conducting.

Bill, I appreciate your time is at a premium but I will make an effort to contact you by phone during the week of June 27th. I look forward to speaking with you in the not too distant future.

Yours truly,

Ray Price

REQUEST FOR A NETWORKING MEETING

ABC COMPANY INC.
1235 - WEST STREET
SOMEWHERE, CANADA L4G 1N2

June 20th, 199_

Attention: Mr. Bill Smith, Director of Marketing

Dear Bill,

First let me introduce myself as we have not met but I wanted to communicate with you regarding some research that I am conducting.

By way of a brief background, I have spent the past 10 years in the _____ industry and I am currently seeking new career options. Let me stress, I am not specifically looking for a position with your organization but I would welcome the opportunity to garner your expert opinion about the macro business strategies being adopted by companies such as ABC.

To be candid, I am gathering this type of information from several sources to aid myself in arriving at some informed personal decisions in terms of viable long-term career objectives.

Bill, I appreciate your time is at a premium but I will call during the week of June 27th. I look forward to speaking with you in the not too distant future.

Yours truly,

Ray Price

FOLLOW UP TO NETWORKING MEETINGS

ABC COMPANY INC.
1235 - WEST STREET
SOMEWHERE, CANADA L4G 1N2

July 20th, 199_

Attention: Mr. Bill Smith, Director of Marketing

Dear Bill,

I simply wanted to drop you a short note to thank you for the time you spent with me on the 19th of July.

As I said during our meeting, I am still in the research phase of my job search but the information you imparted was most helpful. Indeed, your comments regarding _____ were of particular interest.

Bill, I am enclosing a copy of my resume as we discussed and I appreciated the offer to reconnect with you if I had any further questions. Let me also thank you for the suggestion to contact Rob Peters at Dynamic Products Incorporated and I will communicate with him later this week.

I will definitely keep you apprised of my progress.

Yours truly,

Ray Price

SECOND FOLLOW UP TO A NETWORKING MEETING

FORWARDING MATERIAL OF POSSIBLE INTEREST

ABC COMPANY INC.
1235 - WEST STREET
SOMEWHERE, CANADA L4G 1N2

August 15th, 199_

Attention: Mr. Bill Smith, Director of Marketing

Dear Bill,

When we met on July 19th we covered a number of topics and as I recall, you made specific reference to your plans to implement a new initiative known as *Quality 2000*.

While you may have already read the attached article, I felt it addressed several of the issues you raised as potential concerns to your organization. In the event you may have missed seeing it, I thought you would appreciate receiving a copy.

Since we last spoke, I have continued to expand my research in the _____ area and I am certainly concentrating on career options within your sector.

I trust the enclosed information proves to be helpful and I will keep in touch.

Yours truly,

Ray Price

SECOND FOLLOW UP TO A NETWORKING MEETING

OUTLINING SPECIFICS OF CAREER DIRECTION
AND ENCLOSING RESUME

ABC COMPANY INC.
1235 - WEST STREET
SOMEWHERE, CANADA L4G 1N2

August 13th, 199_

Attention: Mr. Bill Smith, Director of Marketing

Dear Bill,

When we met on July 19th I explained that I was in the initial stages of my job search and I was really gathering information to assist me in coming to an informed decision about potential long-term career options.

As expressed before, your input was most helpful and over the course of the past month, I have been able to meet with a wide variety of people who have provided an enormous amount of data. Having now assessed this research in conjunction with a critical review of my own preferences, I have decided to pursue opportunities in the area of _____.

I have taken the liberty of enclosing a final version of my resume and I will definitely keep you posted as to my progress. Again, thank you for taking the time to speak with me last month.

Yours truly,

Ray Price

LETTERS TO PEOPLE IN THE NEWS

ABC COMPANY INC.
1235 - WEST STREET
SOMEWHERE, CANADA L4G 1N2

June 20th, 199_

Attention: Mr. Bill Smith, Director of Marketing

Dear Bill,

First let me introduce myself as we have not met but your quotes in the June 17th Globe were of considerable interest.

Just by way of a brief background, I have spent 10 years in the ___ industry and I am currently looking at potential new career options in that sector. I want to stress, I am not looking for a position with your organization but I would welcome an opportunity to discuss some of the provocative issues you addressed during your interview with the Globe.

I recognize your time is at a premium but I will endeavour to contact you during the week of ____. Perhaps we can review these matters in greater detail when I call.

Yours truly,

Ray Price

DIRECT LETTERS TO TARGETED COMPANIES

ABC COMPANY LTD.
349 CENTRE STREET
SOMEWHERE, CANADA L4G 1N2

June 20th, 199_

Attention: Mr. Gordon Wall - Director of National Sales

Dear Gordon,

Recognizing your time is very valuable, let me move directly to the point of my correspondence.

During the past 15 years I have held progressively senior level positions with an emphasis on _____, within the _____ industry. At the present time, I am seeking out new opportunities. Having conducted preliminary research concerning your organization, I believe my approach to the _____ function aligns with ABC.

I firmly believe my background and credentials would prove to be valuable assets to your firm and while I appreciate you may not have any specific openings at the present time, I expect that you are constantly alert to candidates who could fulfill future requirements.

While the attached resume captures my skills and accomplishments, I have always contended that personality and a proper "fit" with an employer play a major part in the selection process. As such, I would welcome the opportunity to meet with you for a short period of time to allow you to formulate some personal opinions, while posing any questions relative to my past experience and future aspirations.

I will be in touch with you by phone during the week of June 27th and I look forward to speaking with you in the not too distant future.

Yours truly,

Ray Price

LETTERS TO SEARCH FIRMS

S & T PARTNERS INC.
6767 - NORTH AVENUE - SUITE 3000
SOMEWHERE, CANADA L4G 1N2

June 20th, 199_

Attention: Mr. Frank Hall, Partner

Dear Frank,

Recognizing your time is very valuable, let me move directly to the point of my correspondence.

During the past 15 years I have held a variety of progressively senior level positions with a strong emphasis on _____ within the _____ industry. At the present time, I am seeking out new opportunities and the attached resume more specifically addresses and defines my career objectives.

I firmly believe my background and credentials would prove to be valuable assets to a number of potential employers which have engaged your services.

While my resume captures my skills and accomplishments, I have always contended that personality and a proper "fit" with a potential employer play a major part in the selection process. As such, I would welcome the opportunity to meet with you for a short period of time to allow you to formulate some personal opinions and to pose any questions relative to my past experience and future aspirations.

I will be in touch with you by phone during the week of June 27th and I look forward to speaking with you in the not too distant future.

Yours truly,

Ray Price

FOLLOW UP TO UNSUCCESSFUL ATTEMPT TO NETWORK

AFTER PHONE CONVERSATION

TUFF COMPANY INC.
5321 - SOUTH STREET
NOWHERE, CANADA L4G 1N2

June 20th, 199_

Attention: Ms. Mary Jones, Director of Sales

Dear Mary,

I simply wanted to follow up on my earlier correspondence and our discussions of ____.

As I indicated, I am in the midst of looking at possible career options within the ____ industry and I do want to re-emphasize the fact that I was not specifically seeking a position with your organization. That said, your comments and observations were most helpful in terms of expanding my understanding of _____.

Perhaps we can reconvene at a later date and as agreed, I am enclosing a copy of my resume, purely for information purposes. Again, thank you for taking the time to speak with me.

Yours truly,

Ray Price

FOLLOW UP TO UNSUCCESSFUL ATTEMPT TO NETWORK

NO PHONE CONVERSATION

TUFF COMPANY INC.
5321 - SOUTH STREET
NOWHERE, CANADA L4G 1N2

June 20th, 199_

Attention: Ms. Mary Jones, Director of Sales

Dear Mary,

I simply wanted to follow up on my recent phone calls and my earlier correspondence of June 1st.

As I indicated in my letter, I am in the midst of looking at possible career options within the _____ industry and I was interested in garnering your general impressions about the changing sales strategies relative to _____. Let me re-emphasize I am not seeking a position with Tuff Company and I would welcome the opportunity to speak with you at some point in the future.

I recognize your time is always at a premium but I will endeavour to reconnect with you by phone during the week of July 17th, 199_.

Yours truly,

Ray Price

RESPONDING TO A CAREER AD

FUTURE CORPORATION LTD.
1256 - WEST STREET
HOPEFUL, CANADA L4G 1N2

June 20th, 199_

Attention: Director of Management Recruitment

Dear Sir or Madam,

Re: Information Systems Senior Planner #93-987

I am writing in response to the subject advertisement which appeared in the June 15th issue of The National Tribune.

Based on the information provided, the position demands the following specialized requirements and as noted below, my background experience and qualifications closely align with all the priority items:

Strategic & Tactical MIS Planning

During the past 6 years, I have led a team of professionals charged with the responsibility of designing MIS strategies for the year 2000, including the implementation of the first phase which was successfully launched this year. All components were adopted, within budget and activated on or before schedule.

Computer Sciences Degree & Work Experience

As evidenced by my resume, I graduated in the upper quartile of my computer science program from UBC and during my 15 year work history I have utilized my Business Administration degree from U of T extensively.

Highly Polished Communication & Presentation Skills

General communication and presentation skills have been honed through practical business applications and via nationally accredited courses.

Strong Organizational Abilities

While spearheading the previously noted MIS project, a high degree of organizational effectiveness ensured the timely and successful execution of each phase of a program which employed 150 personnel and had a budget of 10 million dollars.

In an effort to provide you with a more comprehensive overview of my past accomplishments and capabilities, I have enclosed my resume and I would welcome an opportunity to more thoroughly explore how my talents might be put to optimum use with your organization.

I look forward to speaking with you in the not too distant future and should you have any questions, I may be reached at 416-555-1212.

Yours truly,

Ray Price

FOLLOW UP TO REJECT LETTERS FROM A CAREER AD

TRIGAIN COMPANY INC.
235 - CENTRE STREET
MAYBE, CANADA L4G 1N2

June 20th, 199_

Attention: Mr. Bob Black, Director of Human Resources

Dear Bob,

Re: _____

On July ___ I responded to the subject career ad in <u>The Herald</u> and I recently received your letter indicating that other potential candidates had been short listed for the vacancy.

I appreciated you taking the time to inform me of the decision and while I am disappointed that my qualifications did not meet all of the job requirements, I can understand your rationale. My future career objectives are very definitely geared toward the _____ industry and as such, I would welcome your input and feedback on my approach to securing a position in this sector.

Clearly, your time is at a premium but I will endeavour to reconnect with you during the week of ____. I look forward to speaking with you in the not too distant future.

Yours truly,

Ray Price

PROPOSALS FOR SERVICE

ABC COMPANY INC.
1235 - WEST STREET
SOMEWHERE, CANADA L4G 1N2

June 20th, 199_

Attention: Mr. Bill Smith, Director of Marketing

Dear Bill,

I appreciated you taking the time out of your hectic schedule to meet with me again on __ .

During our preliminary meeting, you conveyed the changing focus of your company and I certainly sensed last week that you are now firmly committed to pressing forward with innovative initiatives which will enhance the bottom line performance of the _____ division.

Having had time to reflect on several of the issues which we discussed and bearing in mind the information I have garnered during my research about the ____ industry, I would like to put forth an exploratory proposal for your consideration.

The attached outline will provide the basics of my suggested course of action. I would like to reconvene at your convenience to expand upon my concepts and to further investigate how these ideas may complement the new thrust of your organization.

Bill, I believe we are on the same wave length concerning the future direction of ABC and I look forward to progressing our discussions to a mutually beneficial conclusion. I will be in touch with you on June 26th to schedule the next meeting.

Yours truly,

Ray Price

THANK YOU LETTERS FOLLOWING AN INTERVIEW

ABC COMPANY INC.
1235 - WEST STREET
SOMEWHERE, CANADA L4G 1N2

June 20th, 199_

Attention: Mr. Jeff Simmons - Director of Human Resources

Dear Jeff,

I simply wanted to thank you for considering me as a candidate for the position
of _____ with ABC.

As I expressed to you during the interview, I am keenly interested in this type
of position and based on the additional information you provided, I am
confident my background skills, as well as my future career aspirations, closely
align with your requirements and expectations.

Again, thank you for your time and as agreed, I will be in touch with you
during the week of June 27th to determine when you will be progressing to the
final selection stage.

Yours truly,

Ray Price

FOLLOW UP TO LANDING

ABC COMPANY INC.
1235 - WEST STREET
SOMEWHERE, CANADA L4G 1N2

June 20th, 199_

Attention: Mr. Bill Smith, Director of Marketing

Dear Bill,

As you may recall, we had an opportunity to meet not that long ago while I was in the midst of researching possible career options.

I said I would keep you apprised about my progress and I wanted to let you know that I will be joining _____ on _____, as their _____. The position aligns perfectly with my career objectives and I am looking forward to the numerous challenges associated with this new opportunity.

Your input was extremely valuable and I wanted to thank you for taking the time to aid me in my job search. If I can be of any assistance in the future, please give me a call and I will forward you my new business card later this month.

Yours truly,

Ray Price

"Give a man a sword and he can fight

the battle but victory is not always his.

Give a man a pen and he can conquer

the world."

- Author Unknown

APPENDIX

GRAPHICS & FORMS

FOCUS

The adjustment necessary to produce a clear and sharply defined image or area of concentration.

ORGANIZATION

To put in a state of mental competence to perform a task in a well coordinated, consistent, harmonious and systematized fashion.

RESEARCH

To diligently, systematically and carefully inquire or investigate a subject in order to discover or revise facts, theories and applications.

ACTIVITY

The quality of acting promptly, with energy, liveliness, alertness and vigorous action.

FUTURE FOCUS

START

FOCUS

DEALING WITH DEPARTURE, FAMILY ISSUES
FINANCIAL, LEGAL, SETTLEMENTS
ASSESSMENT, SELF ASSESSMENT
ABILITIES / SKILLS REVIEW
ACCOMPLISHMENTS
STRENGTHS

ORGANIZATION   CAREER OBJECTIVE (S)

RESEARCH   RESUME (S)
BUSINESS PLAN

ACTIVITY

SEARCH STRATEGY, CAMPAIGN PLAN
VERIFICATION, FOCUS ADJUSTMENT
INTERVIEWING TECHNIQUES
NEGOTIATING, INTERVIEWS
RESEARCH, NETWORKING
INFORMATION MEETINGS
LETTER WRITING
CAREER ADS

LANDING

ON GOING CAREER MANAGEMENT

P&A 91

NETWORKING DIRECTORY

CONTACT NAME & PHONE #	TITLE	COMPANY	REFERRED BY	PRIORITY RANKING	COMMENTS
1.					
2.					
3.					
4.					
5.					
6.					

NETWORKING DIRECTORY SUPPLEMENT

NAME OF PRIMARY CONTACT:
TITLE: PHONE #
COMPANY:
ADDRESS:
POSTAL CODE:
GENERAL PHONE #:   FAX:

OTHER CONTACTS WITHIN COMPANY			
NAMES	TITLE	REFERRED BY:	PHONE
1.			
2.			
3.			
NOTES:			

AD ANALYZER

DETAILS

-Company name:
-Division:
-Address - Mail:
-Address - Street:
-Fax #:
-Reference #:
-Contact person and title:
-Phone number:
-Title of advertised position:
-Salary range:
-Benefits:
-Job location (s):
-Agents:
-Deadlines:
-Salary expectations:

"CRITICAL REQUIREMENTS"

-Experience:
-Education:
-Skills / Abilities:
-Mobility:
-Languages:
-Computer knowledge:
-Professional affiliations:
-Travel requirements:

AD ANALYZER - CONTINUED

"PREFERRED REQUIREMENTS"

-Experience:
-Education:
-Skills / Abilities
-Mobility:
-Languages:
-Computer knowledge:
-Professional affiliations:
-Travel requirements:

COMPANY BACKGROUND INFORMATION

-Mission Statement:
-Company direction:
-Key descriptive words used in ad:
        -Expansion / Contraction
        -Reorganization / Revitalization
        -Entrepreneurial
        -Market driven
        -Retrenching
        -Leadership
        -Control
        -Work-out scenario
        -Merger / acquisition oriented
        -Sales focus
        -Results-oriented
        -Bottom line driven
        -Pro-active
        -North American focus
        -Global
        -Others_____
        -Others_____

THOMAS INTERNATIONAL

MANAGEMENT SYSTEMS LTD.

In Chapter Five, it was suggested you may want to consider acquiring some form of behavioral evaluation to assist you in completing your own self-assessment.

Many such vehicles are available on the market today but I would like to thank Sean Magennis of Thomas International for providing the following partial sample evaluation. This example includes a basic analysis, as well as special audits in the areas of Management, Administration and Sales. The output you see on the next few pages was derived solely from the responses on the PPA form (see next page), as completed by our fictional character, Mr. Raymond Price.

In addition to the information illustrated in this book, Ray Price could have also chosen to receive other information, including:

-       How to more effectively manage "Mr. Price"
-       Interview questions to be posed to "Mr. Price"
-       Strengths and limitations summary
-       Key issues for "Mr. Price"

The four areas noted above would clearly be of great interest to an existing or future employer. If you are armed with this feedback, you not only achieve greater insight about yourself but you are also in a much stronger position in terms of interview situations. Taking the concept a step further, you are coincidentally preparing to better manage yourself in your ongoing career.

For complete information concerning the Thomas, write Ink Ink Publishing at the address noted on the Request for More Information Form (see last page).

THE PERSONAL PROFILE ANALYSIS

PLEASE PRINT   DATE: _____

SURNAME: _____ ☐ MALE ☐ FEMALE

FORENAMES: _____

COMPANY: _____

PRESENT/LAST POSITION HELD: _____

ADDRESS: _____

_____ WORK/HOME TEL NO.: _____

DIRECTIONS:

Each of the following rectangles contains four descriptive words. Examine the words in the first rectangle and give your first spontaneous reaction. Place an **M** in the box to the right of the word if that is what you are most. Place an L in the box to the right of the Word if that is what you are least. For every four words you should have one **M** and one **L**. The individual in the example to the right perceives of himself as most original and least gentle of the four descriptive words. **Use ball point pen. Please press hard.**

REMEMBER:

1. The analysis is not a test. There are no 'right or 'wrong' answers.

2. The profile must be completed in isolation and without interruption.

3. **Be certain you complete the Personal Profile thinking of yourself in your current job** if you are not working, then think of yourself in your last job. If you have not worked, then think of yourself at home.

© **COPYING OF FORMS IS AN OFFENCE**

THOMAS INTERNATIONAL
MANAGEMENT SYSTEMS LTD

≈ SIXTY FOUR PRINCE ARTHUR AVENUE
TORONTO, CANADA
M5R 1B4 ☎ (416) 920-7702 FAX (416) 920-3165
≈ SUITE 1140 - 1090 WEST GEORGIA STREET
VANCOUVER, B.C.
V6E 3V7 ☎ (604) 684-6678 FAX (604) 684-2579

©1972 Thomas Management Systems Inc.
Revised 1981 Thomas International Management Systems (Europe) Ltd

EXAMPLE

gentle	⌗	persuasive	☐	humble	☐	original	⌗
gentle	☐	persuasive	☐	humble	☐	original	☐
attractive	☐	dutiful	☐	stubborn	☐	sweet	☐
easily led	☐	bold	☐	loyal	☐	charming	☐
open-minded	☐	obliging	☐	will power	☐	cheerful	☐
jovial	☐	precise	☐	courageous	☐	even-tempered	☐
competitive	☐	considerate	☐	happy	☐	harmonious	☐
fussy	☐	obedient	☐	unyielding	☐	playful	☐
brave	☐	inspiring	☐	submissive	☐	timid	☐
sociable	☐	patient	☐	self-reliant	☐	soft-spoken	☐
adventurous	☐	receptive	☐	cordial	☐	moderate	☐
talkative	☐	controlled	☐	conventional	☐	decisive	☐
polished	☐	daring	☐	diplomatic	☐	satisfied	☐
aggressive	☐	gregarious	☐	unsuspecting	☐	fearful	☐
cautious	☐	determined	☐	convincing	☐	good-natured	☐
willing	☐	eager	☐	agreeable	☐	high spirited	☐
confident	☐	sympathetic	☐	tolerant	☐	assertive	☐
well disciplined	☐	generous	☐	lively	☐	persistent	☐
admirable	☐	kind	☐	resigned	☐	forceful	☐
respectful	☐	pioneering	☐	optimistic	☐	accommodating	☐
argumentative	☐	adaptable	☐	relaxed	☐	light-hearted	☐
trusting	☐	contented	☐	positive	☐	peaceful	☐
good mixer	☐	cultured	☐	vigorous	☐	lenient	☐
companionable	☐	accurate	☐	outspoken	☐	restrained	☐
restless	☐	neighbourly	☐	popular	☐	faithful	☐

Thomas International

Management Systems Ltd

PRIVATE AND CONFIDENTIAL

THOMAS INTERNATIONAL MANAGEMENT SYSTEMS

PERSONAL PROFILE ANALYSIS

FOR

Mr. Ray Price

SIXTY FOUR PRINCE ARTHUR AVENUE TORONTO, ONTARIO
CANADA M5R 1B4 TEL (416) 969-7218 FAX (416) 920-3165

OFFICES IN 33 COUNTRIES

THOMAS INTERNATIONAL MANAGEMENT SYSTEMS

Personal Profile Analysis

Mr. Ray Price

Ref W17

Self Image Graph III

This is an assertive person who can take a creative idea and make it serve a practical purpose. He uses a direct method but still considers people and can convince them through persuasiveness when necessary. Aggressive and confident, Mr. Price is goal-minded and harnesses people to help attain goals. He generally plans well ahead and integrates activities to assist in getting results. This versatile, eager self starter acts positively in both competitive and social environments.

Mr. Price may be impatient and irritable when things do not happen fast enough, but he is an excellent director of people in achieving results.

Mr. Price seeks earned respect from associates, needs variety and change. He strives for the independence of a wide scope operation and enjoys challenging assignments which will offer the opportunity to move up the management ladder.

Mr. Price requires negotiated commitments on a person-to-person basis and the opportunity to apply drive and freedom of expression.

Self Motivation

Mr. Price wants prestige, authority and position. He likes to run an operation where tangible, measurable results can be shown and progress can be demonstrated. Seeks earned respect from associates.

Job Emphasis

Managing Work and People for a Profit

Mr. Price's job should ideally require tangible results to be obtained through people. The individual should be under pressure to produce and frequently be required to apply pressure to others. Planning, problem solving and organising should be key responsibilities. Authority to make decisions and the independence to act should be vested in Mr. Price, as well as the need to delegate to others. The working environment should be relatively unpredictable and should call for several projects to be kept going concurrently.

Although operating policies might exist, Mr. Price should frequently be able to act without a precedent.

Describing Words

Self starter, direct, decisive, demanding, self assured, confident, friendly, verbal, active, mobile, alert, restless, firm, independent, strong willed.

How Others See You (Mask) Graph I

Whilst the low compliance factor in the self image suggests that Mr. Price will be strong-willed and independent, there are clear signs in the work mask that he modifies his behaviour a little in the work situation. At work he may not be quite as strong willed and independent as the self image suggests. This is not likely to have a major effect on his basic characteristics.

Behaviour Under Pressure Graph II

There are clear indicators that when much pressure is placed on Mr. Price he may become very demanding. There are also additional indicators which suggest that if the pressure is maintained, then he may, from time to time, and then only for short periods, reverse characteristics and become more cautious, conservative and milder in manner. This aspect needs consideration as it could create relationship problems in pressure situations.

Under pressure, Mr. Price may lose a little confidence in his persuasive ability, but nevertheless retains a very positive communicative style.

General Comments

Stress

Mr. Price shows no signs of stress within the profile.

This is usually an indicator that he is either behaviourally suited for the position he occupies, or that he can modify his characteristics to suit this position.

Motivators

Mr. Price is naturally motivated by prestige, position, money and material things, challenge and an opportunity for advancement.

He likes to be given freedom from control, unnecessary detail and supervision.

Mr. Price ideally needs a manager who is a direct leader with good people skills if the best relationships are to be achieved. It will be necessary for the manager to ensure that Mr. Price knows what results are expected, the timescales required, and against what standards the performance is to be assessed.

As we have not been given a Human Job Analysis for this post, it has not been possible to make a detailed assessment of Mr. Price's strengths and weaknesses against the specific job requirement. Furthermore, please remember the above document is a guide only; the Personal

Profile Analysis does not take into account intellect, education, experience, seniority, qualifications, product, industry or market exposure. It is a work oriented inventory and must be utilised together with all other available evaluation procedures and techniques.

THOMAS INTERNATIONAL MANAGEMENT SYSTEMS

Career Guidelines For Mr. Ray Price

Ref J13-1

Managerial Entrepreneurial

General Management, (Directing/Managing/Supervising), Public Relations, Industrial Relations, Trouble Shooting, Sales and Sales Management, Marketing and Marketing Management, Promotions, Production (Director, Manager, Supervisor), Consultancy, Self Employment, Advertising, Lecturing and Dealing/Broking.

The above career indicators have been compiled over the past two decades from international and local research. Please remember that they are intended as a guideline only and in no way suggest that these are the only posts to which the HJA could apply.

THOMAS INTERNATIONAL MANAGEMENT SYSTEMS

Management Audit On Mr. Ray Price

Ref M17

Managing and motivating

Mr. Price has natural characteristics for managing and motivating others as well as for achieving a positive and profitable result.

He will certainly identify opportunity, has innovative tendencies and will accept the responsibility of managing and directing via his natural leadership style.

Whilst he will always push people to achieve a result, all the indicators are that in so doing Mr. Price will create very positive attitudes towards success in others.

Mr. Price will be prepared to involve his subordinates in decision taking and will motivate them to feel a valuable member of the team.

Mr. Price is likely to be a good disciplinarian who will discuss people problems with those concerned prior to taking disciplinary action.

Decision making

Being naturally decisive Mr. Price will consider any action which needs to be taken, whenever possible get the facts, and then use his knowledge and experience to make a positive and firm decision. If Mr. Price feels that he has made an incorrect decision, then he will have no difficulty in revising such a decision to get matters back on a profitable course.

Planning and problem solving

Being such a positive individual all the indications are that Mr. Price has an ability to plan if a result depends upon it, and should prove an innovative problem solver.

Mr. Price is both objective and venturesome in solving problems, and is generally likely to provide alternative ideas.

Communication

As a result of his ability to create enthusiasm, the clear indicators are that he will not only make a good impression on other people, but will in addition keep them motivated on a long term basis.

Mr. Price's communication style will rely upon his ability to influence and persuade people as well as his personality. All his communication is likely to be in a positive vein, and will seek the point of view of others.

Administration

Mr. Price is not a particularly good administrator and works best when provided with an administrative backup service. The basic problem is that Mr. Price may not always allow sufficient time to get the administration right, and others may feel that he takes too many short cuts.

It cannot be denied however, that if a result depends upon strong administration, Mr. Price can complete the task.

Developing others

There is no doubt that Mr. Price has good abilities to identify and implement development plans for others.

He is likely to create enthusiasm in both appraisal and development areas and will normally lead the action to implement development programmes.

Mr. Price is likely to feel that profitable progress starts with a strong development structure.

THOMAS INTERNATIONAL MANAGEMENT SYSTEMS

Sales Audit On Mr. Ray Price

Ref S17

Opening and communication

Mr. Price has good opening abilities and creates a positive impression when he comes into contact with new people for the first time.

Mr. Price reflects confidence and has a direct approach which generates enthusiasm and interest in others. He is resourceful in dealing with others and will always appear to identify solutions.

He is a good communicator who has an ability to express his feelings which in turn motivates people toward him.

Mr. Price will use force of character in his communication and is likely to come over as self assured in his product and/or service.

Closing

Being a forceful person, sales closing is a natural behavioural trait for Mr. Price. He will state the case, search for opportunities and try to win people to his way of thinking.

Mr. Price has strong characteristics when it comes to overcoming objections and pushing hard to achieve a positive and profitable result. He is determined to win new orders and has innovative ideas when closing.

There may be occasions when Mr. Price becomes a little too enthusiastic about his product or service and this in turn could cause him to miss buying signs and perhaps appear a little over-powering to those whose characteristics are not as strong as his own.

Customer servicing

Whilst there is no doubt whatsoever that Mr. Price will work very hard at servicing the customer in order to achieve the success that he is looking for, there are also clear indicators that Mr. Price may at times not allow sufficient time for servicing the client.

This can cause him to show impatience with those clients who want to spend much time with him and in those instances there may be a tendency for Mr. Price to neglect to tie up the loose ends and ultimately to fail to service as expected by the client.

Presentation

As a result of Mr. Price's natural influencing and persuasive characteristics, all the indicators suggest that he would be a good presenter. It should also be noted that Mr. Price will improve his presentation as product/service knowledge is gained and it is therefore important to ensure that good product/service training is provided.

Administration

All the indicators are that Mr. Price may have a tendency to neglect to tie up the loose ends. Basically he is a person who enjoys being with and meeting others and as a direct result he may devote too little time to administrative requirements.

If Mr. Price was required to spend considerable time on the organisation of information, there is no doubt that he would become frustrated and his performance would deteriorate.

THOMAS INTERNATIONAL MANAGEMENT SYSTEMS

Administration Audit On Mr. Ray Price

Ref 413

Organising Work Flow

Mr. Price acts with authority. He enjoys having broad parameters within which to work, making his own decisions and creating his own structure. Due to the fact that Mr. Price dislikes detail and routine he will tend to delegate such functions to others. He is likely to be a good communicator and motivator of people and will enlist the enthusiastic co-operation of others.

Mr. Price also enjoys being involved in generalist areas and does not want to be too tied down with paperwork and routine tasks. He can be very enthusiastic at the beginning of a task but his follow through may not always be relied upon.

Meeting Deadlines And Time Management

Mr. Price will respond well to pressure and deadlines but accuracy may be sacrificed in the process of meeting deadlines. He also has a need to participate with others for input and wants to work in a team environment. This may sometimes affect time management and he can become over-involved in aspects not directly related to the task in hand. Due to Mr. Price's interest in others he can at times spend too much time in communicating, both with peers and superiors, and not enough time in getting the actual work done, particularly if the work is perceived as routine or mundane. The strong end result orientation should ensure that deadlines are met.

Meeting Information/Service Needs

Mr. Price tends to selectively meet the needs of clients, depending on whether or not he has built up rapport with those clients. Because he is not fond of dealing with too much detail and facts, information may not always be complete or accurate.

He tends to get carried away with enthusiasm and may sometimes make promises which he cannot meet.

However, he will generally be helpful and friendly.

He will prefer to communicate verbally rather than in the written form.

Ensuring Quality And Accuracy

Mr. Price's impatient, hurried attitude may impact on quality and accuracy and he may therefore have problems in sticking with a task to ensure its completion. He needs a great deal of variety as he is prone to a low boredom threshold. He will tend to depend on others for follow-up in this area. Due to Mr. Price's end result orientation he, whilst not being perfectionistic, will expect quality and accuracy from subordinates.

Problem Solving

Mr. Price enjoys working in a team to reach solutions. However, he also tends to know his own. mind and is independent and creative enough to come up with solutions of his own and often comes up with imaginative, untried solutions. He is not a rational, logical problem solver and Mr. Price relies heavily on intuition to reach solutions. Generally problem solving is Mr. Price's greatest strength.

ORDER BY:

- ## CALLING OR FAXING: 1-800-263-1991

  - ## MAILING TO :
    Christie & Christie Associates
    P.O. Box 392
    Cookstown, Ontario L0L 1L0

Quantity   **Amount**

_____ From Fired..... ....To Hired @ $19.95* _____

*Includes Shipping and GST
- Regular Price at Retail Outlets - $16.95
- Discounts Available for Larger Volumes

Name:	
Address:	
City:	Province:
Postal Code:	

Method of Payment:

_____ My cheque or money order is enclosed for the above total.

_____ Please invoice me for the above total.

_____ Please charge my Visa, Master Card* or American Express*:

Account Number: ___ ___ ___ ___ ___ ___ ___ ___ ___ ___ ___ ___ ___

Signature Authorizing Purchase_____Expiry Date _____
*Only applicable to fax or mail orders.

Ink Ink Publishing
Phone: 416-230-3241

REQUEST FOR MORE INFORMATION

Thomas International
Management Systems Ltd.

Ink Ink Publishing
120 Promenade Circle - Suite 1107
Thornhill, Ontario
Canada   L4J 7W9
Phone: 416-230-3241

Without obligation, please send me more detailed information regarding the Thomas International behavioral assessments. The material may be forwarded to the following address:

Name	
Address	
City	Province
Postal Code	